T0329016

 # Card Decks

CAR GO CARDS: *Fabulously Foolproof On-the-Road Activities for Fidgety Kids,* from the Publishers of *Parenting®* magazine

RAINY-DAY FUN CARDS: *Easy Indoor Games and Activities Your Kids Will Love,* from the Publishers of *Parenting®* magazine

All of the above are available at your local bookstore, or may be ordered by visiting:

Hay House USA: **www.hayhouse.com®**
Hay House Australia: **www.hayhouse.com.au**
Hay House UK: **www.hayhouse.co.uk**
Hay House India: **www.hayhouseindia.co.in**

sign, sing, and play!

Fun Signing Activities for You and Your Baby

by Monta Z. Briant

HAY HOUSE, INC.
Carlsbad, California • New York City
London • Sydney • New Delhi

Published in the United States by: Hay House, Inc.: www.hayhouse.com
Published in Australia by: Hay House Australia Pty. Ltd.: www.hayhouse.com.au
Published in the United Kingdom by: Hay House UK, Ltd.: www.hayhouse.co.uk
Published in India by: Hay House Publishers India: www.hayhouse.co.in

Editorial supervision: Jill Kramer • *Design:* Jenny Richards • *Interior photos of Monta:* Greg Bertolini • *Photos of children:* Paul Briant, Susan Zelinsky, Mike Jobe, Mike Zelinsky, and Jennifer Vignale • *I Love You Hand and Foot Photos:* Bill Pitcher • *Illustrations:* Diana Hocking, www.dianahocking.com

The author of this book does not dispense medical advice or prescribe the use of any technique as a form of treatment for physical, emotional, or medical problems without the advice of a physician, either directly or indirectly. The intent of the author is only to offer information of a general nature to help you in your quest for emotional and spiritual well-being. In the event you use any of the information in this book for yourself, which is your constitutional right, the author and the publisher assume no responsibility for your actions.

Library of Congress Control Number: 2005936318

Tradepaper ISBN: 978-1-4019-6949-3

1st printing, July 2006
2nd printing, August 2006

Printed in the United States of America

For my new little signer, Aiden, aka "Mr. Personality";

my big signing girl, Sirena, who trained me
rigorously in how to sign with babies;

my wonderful husband, Paul,
the world's greatest and most patient husband;

and my dad, Mike Zelinsky, aka "His Lordship,
Lord Plywood" for giving me the "writing bug."

You are my inspiration!

contents

PART III: THE SIGNS

APPENDIX

preface

When I started signing with my first child, Sirena, I had no previous experience using this form of language. I was a little bit dubious about the whole idea—and many of you reading this can probably relate! The possibility of being able to communicate with my infant intrigued me, however, so I decided to give it a try.

Once my baby started signing back to me, I was ecstatic—it was so incredible to see Sirena expressing her thoughts and needs in a way that I could clearly understand. I became a huge advocate of this process—a "baby sign language evangelist," if you will—chasing down anyone pushing a stroller. Soon, I started offering classes in the

San Diego area, where I live (much more efficient than stroller-chasing), and not long afterward I wrote my own book on the topic, *Baby Sign Language Basics: Early Communication for Hearing Babies and Toddlers.*

In the early stages of signing with my daughter, I mostly focused on communicating at mealtimes, when nursing, and occasionally during diaper changes. I soon began to get bored with this, and as a result, I decided that I needed to find more meaningful and creative ways to include signing in our daily routine. So, I started to invent a few games and activities for us to sign along with.

I was amazed by how quickly Sirena learned in the context of playtime. She appeared much more attentive when I signed to her, and began adding to her vocabulary in leaps and bounds! Soon after, when I began teaching other parents, I took this process further as I developed the curriculum to use in my classes.

Since writing *Baby Sign Language Basics,* we've welcomed another baby into our family: our son, Aiden. It's so exciting to be embarking on this journey again, armed with all that I learned the first time around! I have had the advantage of being able to use everything I learned the first time around, right from the start. As a result, Aiden produced his first sign at just less than six months of age, even earlier than I *started* signing to Sirena. At 9 months, Aiden was intermittently using more than a dozen signs, and by 14 months he was consistently signing more than 60 words and concepts in order to communicate his needs and express his interests and observations.

My fellow teachers, students, and signing parents have generously contributed many of their own ideas for this book, for which I'm very grateful. And as you read, you'll also probably find yourself inspired with new ideas of your own. Have fun, and happy signing!

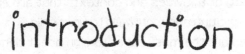

introduction

Parents who have the most success in signing
with their babies have figured out the number one secret to signing success: *Babies sign
earlier and use signs more frequently if parents make
the experience fun and motivating!*

In the pages ahead, you'll find dozens of fun and
engaging signing activities for babies and toddlers.
I've grouped the activities by chapter according to
the type of situation you could use them in, such
as "Creative Signing with Daily Routines," "Signing
While Out and About," and "Signing with Toys." Most
of the activities are very easy to incorporate into
your daily routine, which is the whole point. As you

read this book, you may find yourself saying, "Why didn't I think of that?" The idea is to include signing every day, in a variety of activities and contexts that are easy for you, yet exciting and *motivating* to your child.

Babies are the most eager to sign about things that they're very interested in and curious about, yet can't express by crying. The question you need to ask yourself is: *If my baby could talk right now, what would he want to say?*

Consider the following examples:

- "Mommy, what's that animal?"
- "Daddy, that truck makes a loud noise!"
- "Please sing to me more!"
- "Look! There are bright lights over there!"
- "I hear a dog barking!"

These are typical of the kinds of things that babies want to say but usually have no way to communicate. Can you imagine an infant trying to express these ideas by crying? That just wouldn't do the trick.

Here's an example from my own experience: I diligently used the sign **MILK** with my second baby every time I nursed, right from the day he was born. By the time he was nine months old, I was beginning to feel frustrated, because although he clearly recognized the sign, he wouldn't use it to tell me he wanted to nurse, opting to cry instead. One day at the natural-history museum, my son spotted a picture of a topless prehistoric Indian woman. He immediately began signing **MILK** frantically, with both hands!

What made the difference? He could cry to say, "I want milk," but that wouldn't be appropriate to communicate, "Hey! Look at those!"

When using this book, watch for words in **BOLD CAPS,** as they represent signed words. Additional suggested signs are highlighted with a book icon: and can be found in Part III.

For even more fun ways to include signing with your baby, be sure to check the Resources section, which includes American Sign Language (ASL) board books, DVDs and videos, and music CDs for kids, as well as other learning materials such as flash cards and ASL dictionaries. To get more signs online, go to the ASL Browser Website, **http://commtechlab.msu.edu/sites/aslweb/index. htm,** to see a QuickTime video of just about any sign you can think of. It's fun, and it's free!

You and your baby are about to embark on one of the most exciting journeys you will ever share. Cherish every minute of it!

In Part I, we're going to review some of the basics of signing with babies. If you've recently read my first book, *Baby Sign Language Basics*, you may want to go on to Part II. If you haven't read it yet, or if you did so a couple of years ago with your first child, be aware that this section is only intended to give you a brief overview of how to sign with your baby. In order to get the best results, it's best to read *Baby Sign Language Basics* in its entirety. (It's a tiny book—a very quick read!)

[**Author's Note:** In order to avoid the awkward he/she construction, I have opted to alternate the use of the masculine and feminine pronoun throughout this book. Please note that the same information applies universally to both girls and boys.]

part I

baby
sign language
basics

Chapter 1

What? Why? When? How?

What Is "Baby Sign Language" Anyway?

Baby sign language is the practice of using symbolic gestures to enhance your verbal interactions with your child. All human beings naturally use meaningful motions. Imagine your baby lifting her arms to be picked up or pointing at something to draw your attention to it. Just as she learns to wave "Bye-bye" or shrug her shoulders to ask "What?" from seeing you do so, your baby can also learn to use American Sign Language gestures (signs) to communicate her needs, express her interests, and ask questions long before she can talk.

3

Why Should I Sign with My Hearing Baby?

Having open, two-way communication with your child makes life so much easier for both of you—and besides, it's just so much *fun* to know what he's trying to tell you!

Signing with your baby also:

- Enhances bonding

- Decreases crying and tantrums

- Accelerates verbal-language acquisition

- Stimulates interest in books—your baby can comment on and name objects in pictures!

- Raises self-esteem

- Increases IQ [1]

- Gives you a window into your child's thoughts and feelings

With all these benefits, why *wouldn't* you sign with your hearing baby?

You can begin using signs at any age, but six to seven months old is considered the earliest optimal starting time. Parents who start at this time can reasonably expect their babies to sign back when they're between eight and ten months of age. Older babies and toddlers—say ten months and up—usually catch on more quickly, and may sign back in just a few weeks.

It's important to realize that before they reach six months, infants have very little long-term memory, so it will take them longer to sign back. Babies younger than six or seven months also lack the motor skills and hand-eye coordination required to make precise movements, so parents may miss these early signing attempts (perceiving them as random gestures) or find that all of the signs seem to look alike.

I started this process at six months with my first child and signed from birth with my second. Here's what I discovered with my two children (which is, of course, by no means a scientific study!):

- **Baby #1:** I started signing to Sirena at six months, and she first signed back at nine months. It took her three months to produce her first sign.

- **Baby #2:** I started signing to Aiden as soon as he was born, and it took him five months and three weeks to produce his first sign.

All in all, I have to say that I don't think starting from birth made a huge difference in Aiden's preverbal communicative ability. Although he started signing when he was several months younger than his sister had been, it still took him several *more* months to really rely upon signing instead of crying. By 14 months, Aiden had nearly 60 signs—only a few more than Sirena did at the same age.

One thing that I *did* find helpful in starting earlier was that my son clearly recognized many of *my* signs and spoken words at a very early age. At just three months old, my son would respond to both the signs and spoken words **TICKLE** (by grinning and wriggling) and **MILK** (by crying). He'd even do this in his sleep (in response to the spoken words, of course, not the signs!).

Because your baby will recognize and respond to your gestures long before she can sign them back, you'll definitely experience some rewards for your efforts, even while you wait for that first recognizable sign.

How Do I Sign with My Baby?

Signing with your baby is different from just plain talking to him and requires some different strategies. There are specific ways to get him to see what you're doing, as well as methods to reinforce the meaning of your signs and spoken words.

— Get on your baby's level. You should be doing this when you interact with your child verbally, too. Get right down on the floor with her; hold her in your arms or lap or sit across from her when she's in her high chair.

— Sign in your baby's field of vision. Usually, this means signing close to your face, just below your line of sight. Babies are naturally attracted to the human face, and they'll be looking in the direction that the talking is coming from. (There are some exceptions to this, especially during playtime, which we'll discuss in Chapter 3.)

— Say the word. When signing with hearing babies, it's extremely important to always say the word when you sign it. Ultimately, you want your child to learn to recognize the spoken word without your signing it, and later to learn to say the word himself. This will happen more easily if he makes a strong connection between the verbal sounds and the gestures.

7

— **Sign in context.** When your baby is first learning a new sign, she needs to experience it *in context* in order to make a clear association. For example, don't sign about the **BEAR** you saw yesterday at the zoo. Instead, sign about the **BEAR** *while* you're watching it. Daddy may point at it while saying and signing: "Hey! Look at the **BEAR!** What a big, fluffy **BEAR!**" Alternatively, you could also sign about a **BEAR** in a book or a teddy **BEAR.**

— **Teach motivating signs.** That's what this book is all about! Babies are motivated to communicate their needs, desires, interests, feelings, and observations, and often these are things that they can't express by crying. The signs they'll learn most quickly are the ones that are the most fun for them. Signs such as **AIRPLANE, LIGHT, FAN,** and **DOG,** for example, are very motivating to most babies.

"Routine" signs, such as **MORE,** can be very motivating when used in certain contexts: **MORE MUSIC, MORE PLAY, MORE TICKLE,** and so on. Similarly, utilitarian signs such as **DIAPER CHANGE** or **EAT** can be made more fun when used in playtime. For example, as you have fun with a teddy bear, you can say, "Let's give Teddy a **DIAPER CHANGE** and some food to **EAT.**"

— **Accompany the sign with the appropriate facial expression.** Often, the facial expression is just as important as the hand shape. The gesture for **SCARED,** for example, is accompanied by a startled look. Imagine if you smiled while doing this sign—it wouldn't convey the same meaning at all!

There isn't always an obvious facial expression for a sign. For example, what expression goes with **MILK?** Well, if you're nursing your baby, you might hold your hand close to your face and sign **MILK** while saying "Mmm, that's good **MILK!**" You'd probably smile while saying this, since that would be the natural expression for commenting on something being good.

Now, if you were offering **MILK,** however—saying "Do you want **MILK?**" you would raise your eyebrows into a "questioning face" and exaggerate the querying tone of your voice. When you do this, your baby is not only learning the sign for **MILK,** but is also gaining another valuable language skill: what a question looks and sounds like.

— **Most important . . . keep it fun!** The most essential thing to remember when signing with your baby is to keep it fun and lighthearted—don't stress out about whether or not he seems to be paying attention to you, and don't worry if he isn't signing back as quickly as you think he should.

Children pick up on your tension very easily, and if they associate these interactions with stress, they won't want to participate. Teach the skills the same way that you teach him to wave bye-bye or sing "The Itsy Bitsy Spider." Signing should *enhance* your normal playtime without being intrusive. Believe me, just when you think your child will never sign back to you—pop! Out of the blue comes that first sign, and then the next and the next. Hang in there—your baby *will* sign!

chapter 2

The Importance of Signing with Playtime

Most of us just can't wait for our baby to actually start signing back to us! We diligently repeat the same signs over and over again, trying to keep the faith until that magic day when her hands finally come together in an attempt to convey meaning. If you want your child to start signing back to you as soon as possible, the single most effective thing you can do is to include signing with playtime!

Playing engages and stimulates little minds like nothing else, and when signing is added into the equation, the fun is multiplied! Take songs like "Where is Thumbkin?"

"The Wheels on the Bus," or "The Itsy Bitsy Spider," for example. Babies love these songs with gestures, because the movements give them a way to participate long before they can talk or sing the words themselves.

Signing not only enriches playtime, but it can also be used to make everyday activities more fun. One of the biggest mistakes parents make is that they often neglect to use signs that are fun and motivating to their babies.

When I decided to begin this process with my first child, Sirena, I thought that the greatest benefit was going to be her ability to express her basic needs by signing instead of crying. So, being the practical person that I am, I diligently began using only the signs that I thought were the most "useful" and "important": **MILK, MORE,** and **EAT.** I started doing this with Sirena when she was six months old and was very consistent about including the signs at every nursing and mealtime.

I must admit that I wasn't very imaginative in how and when I used these gestures. For example, I initially only thought of signing **MORE** and **EAT** in the context of feeding my daughter rice cereal, which she was mostly spitting out anyway in the early stages. There sat Mommy on the other side of her high-chair tray, asking and signing, "Do you want **MORE?**" as Sirena spat out her cereal and thought, *Yuck! What is this stuff? Where's my milk?*

Because my little girl wasn't wild about solids yet, she wasn't experiencing a keen longing for **FOOD (EAT)** or **MORE,** and so she wasn't motivated to use those signs. Because she didn't *want* more, she probably didn't even make the connection between the sign for **MORE** and its true meaning.

Through my experience in signing with Sirena, I learned an important lesson: Babies will be much more motivated to sign for things that are fun and interesting to *them.* They'll also be more interested in learning signs for things that they want to express but can't communicate by crying or whining. Often, this means that the baby's first sign won't be something that the parent thinks is important, such as **DIAPER CHANGE** or **MILK,** but rather something that the child is really interested in, such as **AIRPLANE** or **DOG.**

As Sirena began expanding her signing vocabulary, I figured out something else: It's possible to incorporate the more utilitarian signs into playful situations, thereby making them more motivating to baby. For example, you can give the child's favorite stuffed animal or doll a **DIAPER CHANGE** or some **MILK,** thus including these "routine" concepts in playtime.

As I began using signs in more entertaining ways and stopped being so darned serious about the whole thing, my daughter's signing vocabulary increased in leaps and bounds. By the time Sirena was 15 months old, she was using nearly 60 signs and eventually learned more than 200 of them.

When I began offering parent/child Sign, Sing, and Play classes in 2002, I employed the "playtime principles" I'd learned while working with my daughter and designed the program to be primarily "play focused." In these sessions, I teach parents to include signing naturally in fun ways during various activities throughout their day. While singing songs, playing with toys, and playing games, they not only learn to sign during playtime, but also with potty time, bath time, mealtime, story time, and bedtime.

I often have parents come to my classes who have been signing to their child for several months without success. Many times they call me up after just one meeting to tell me that their baby began signing several new words that very same day—and not the ones that the parents had been diligently working on all those months, but *new* signs from the class!

Sometimes, introducing signs in a way that appears "just for fun" to the baby is all it takes to finally get them interested. With my second child, Aiden, I had the opportunity to use the playful approach from the beginning in my own household. I started using the sign for **MORE** as soon as he was born, and because he wasn't eating solid foods yet, I had to come up with other ways to include the sign meaningfully. I began by doing something I knew he enjoyed, such as tickling or singing. Now and then I'd stop momentarily and ask, "Do you want **MORE?**" I'd wait for a moment, as if for a response from him, and then tickle or sing some more.

Very quickly, Aiden learned to recognize the signs *and spoken words* for **MORE** and **TICKLE.** At barely three months old, he'd even respond to the spoken words in his sleep—smiling at the word *tickle* and waking up and crying when he heard the word *milk.* And at just under six months, he began signing for **MORE** himself.

Aiden's next two signs were **LIGHT** and **FAN.** I'd introduced these words early on, because as most parents can attest, these things are really fascinating to babies. They spend a lot of time lying down and looking up, so they really notice what's on the ceiling! So when choosing the first signs to use with your baby, it's a good idea to try to picture the world from his perspective. For example, what does he see when he's looking up? What does he see when he's crawling? Get down on the floor and crawl around, and lie on your back while looking around the room. What do you see in your baby's world? Probably a lot of great stuff to sign about!

Now just how do you get your baby to actually pay attention and see you signing when she's more interested in looking at all those other fascinating things? That's the topic of the next chapter!

Chapter 3

Getting Baby to See Your Signs

So there you are, spending some quality time sign-ing and playing with your baby. The two of you are playing with his "busy box," and he's just pushed the button that makes the little bear come out. You're signing **BEAR** repeatedly, and your child seems to be totally focused on . . . his busy box. He's completely absorbed in the toy, and he absolutely won't look at you signing **BEAR.** What should you do?

In this chapter, I've provided some attention-getting strategies from my first book, *Baby Sign Language Basics.* Even if you've previously read it, you may want to review these techniques, as they're especially useful and important for signing during playtime.

Many of these ideas have come from watching deaf mothers interact with their babies. Just as hearing parents raise the pitch of their voices to get their child's attention, deaf parents modify their signing and use various other tactics while interacting with their babies.

— **Verbal attention getting.** Call your child's name or use a term of endearment: "Hey, Pun'kin, look at Mommy!"

— **Seize the moment.** Sometimes you and your baby will just look at each other spontaneously, for no particular reason. This is what *Sign with Your Baby* author Joseph Garcia calls the "chance mutual gaze." When this happens, you can just grab a nearby toy or another object that might interest your baby and model the sign for it. For example, ask: "Do you want your **(BALL, BOOK, BEAR)**?"

— **Lie in wait.** Sometimes, the best way to get your baby to look at you is to do nothing at all. If you sit there watching her play, she'll look up at you from time to time as if to say, "Are you *still* sitting there watching me?" This is what Garcia terms the "expressive gaze," which is when your baby wants to express a feeling or ask a question.[1] This is the perfect time to sign about whatever it is she's playing with. For example, you might say "You have your **DOGGY!** Are you biting your **DOGGY**'s nose?"

— **Share experiences spontaneously.** Often, you and your baby will look at the same thing, and then at each other. This is what Garcia terms the "pointed gaze," and now that you know about it, you'll notice it happening a lot. Imagine that you're out for a walk with your baby, and a crow squawks loudly from the overhead wire. You'd both probably look up at the bird and then at each other, as if to say, "Did you hear that?" This would be a perfect time to say and sign **HEAR,** and then point at the crow and say and sign **BIRD.**

— **Get physical.** Videotapes of deaf mothers interacting with their children show the women actively seeking their babies' attention by gently but persistently tapping their hands or other parts of their bodies.[2] Tapping your child's hands when you want him to sign back reminds him that there's something you expect him to do with his hands. You can also stroke or rub your child to get his attention; touching his cheek with a finger will often get him to turn toward you.

In Chapter 1, I recommended that you sign close to your face and in your baby's field of vision—but with infants, these two things don't always go together. Although it's best to allow your baby to see the object of interest and your sign at same time, at first you'll find that this is easier said than done. The following additional strategies, reprinted from *Baby Sign Language Basics,* are suggested by Michelle Anthony and Reyna Lindert of Wide-Eyed Learning, who use these methods in their *Signing Smart* parent/child classes. (They've since published these ideas in their book, *Signing Smart with Babies and Toddlers,* St. Martin's Griffin, May 2005.)

— Sign on your child's body. With some signs, it's just as effective for the child to feel the sensation of the gesture on their body as it is to actually see it; **DOG** is a great example. If your child is looking at a dog or listening to one barking, you could sign **DOG** on her thigh rather than your own (it involves slapping the thigh as if calling the animal). Clearly, the baby doesn't need to look at her leg to know what's happening. Some other signs that work well with this technique are **BEAR, COW,** and **TELEPHONE.**

— Produce the sign in front of your child's body. This is easy to do when the baby is facing you, but can also be done when he has his back to you. Reach around as if you're hugging him from behind, and produce your sign either on or in front of his body. This works well for signs such as **BEAR** and **MORE**.

— Move the sign into your child's line of sight. This is what Anthony and Lindert term "displacing" your sign.[3] To do this, simply move so that you're signing between the baby's body and the object she's looking at. This works well with signs that only require the use of your hands, such as **BALL** and **KEY**.

— Bring the object of interest toward you. Pick up the thing that interests your child and bring it toward your upper body, then produce the sign for it. The baby's gaze will usually follow the object until it rests in front of you, allowing him to see it and your sign at the same time. You can also gently take the object from him, bring it toward yourself, produce your sign, and then give it back to him. Don't force him to relinquish a toy if he doesn't want to, however, and *always* return it.

— Sign to your child's perspective. Because your baby is a little person, she often sees your signs from below. While the first choice is to get on her level to sign, this isn't always possible. Sometimes a busy mommy's knees just say "No!" In this case, think about how she'll see your sign and angle it so that she sees it "head-on."

Now that you've reviewed some of the basics, it's time to play! The next chapter is filled with activities that make it fun and easy to sign throughout the day.

part II

fun
signing
activities

Chapter 4

Signing Around the House

As parents, we often get stuck on just signing at predetermined times, such as diapering and mealtimes. This can get old pretty fast. In order to keep baby (and you!) interested, it's a good idea to include signing in fresh and interesting ways throughout the day. Anytime you're talking to or interacting with your baby, there's probably also a sign that you could be showing him—you just need to use your imagination a little and think outside the box. Even ordinary occurrences can be made into signing games, many of which only take a moment to play.

My son, Aiden, and daughter, Sirena, signing SEAL.

In this chapter we'll explore ways to use signs with ordinary household objects and occurrences. Some of these are activities that you can sit down and play for several minutes, while others are fun things that you can just do in passing as you go through your day. Doing them with your baby will help make signing an integrated part of her world. By signing in various situations throughout the day, she'll begin to make an exciting discovery: All of life is an adventure, and *everything* has a sign!

You'll find one or two appropriate sign illustrations with each activity. And remember that when you see a book icon, , it means that additional suggested signs can be found in the "Signing Vocabulary" section in Part III.

✻ ✻ ✻

There's No Place Like Home

The sign for **HOME** is more motivating to babies than you might think. Soon after I used this sign with Aiden for the first time, he began employing it when we were out running errands, telling me that he was tired and wanted to go home!

The sign for **HOUSE** is different from **HOME,** since it can apply to anyone's house, rather than where your family lives.

What to Do

- Sign **HOME** each time you arrive at the house with him, making the movements as you get him out of the car seat or stroller.

- Use **HOUSE** to refer to your own residence, friend's places, dollhouses, and pictures of houses.

- **HOUSE** is even applicable for birdhouses or doghouses when it's accompanied by the appropriate animal sign! Using it in a variety of contexts teaches your baby that there are different kinds of houses.

HOME. The fingers and thumb, brought together to form an "O," move from the side of the mouth to the cheek. This is a variation of **EAT** and **SLEEP.**

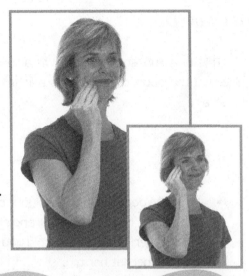

HOUSE. The flat hands describe an outline of a house with a pointed roof.

29

Ring the Doorbell

This is a fun activity that will also give you the opportunity to get a little fresh air.

What to Do

- With the door open so that your baby can hear the sound, ring the doorbell and sign **HEAR** and **BELL** to her, while asking, "Did you **HEAR** the **BELL?**" Then let her try.

- If your child needs assistance pushing or reaching the bell, ask if she needs **HELP,** and then give her a hand.

- She'll definitely want to do this more than once, so be sure to ask, "Do you want to ring the **BELL MORE** (or **AGAIN**)?"

- Play until you've had enough . . . or the doorbell breaks!

 **AGAIN, HELP, LISTEN,** and **MORE**

BELL. The right hand is held facing down with the wrist bent and fingertips and thumb close together, representing a bell shape. The palm of the open left hand strikes the bell twice.

HEAR. The natural gesture: The index finger points to the ear. You may observe your baby doing this naturally in response to sounds, even before you do it.

Talking on the Telephone

Babies are fascinated by the telephone. They see us big people use it a lot, so they think that the phone must be a lot of fun—and they can't wait to get their hands on it!

What to Do

- Whenever you use the phone, sign **TELEPHONE.**

- When it rings, you can sign **TELEPHONE** and/or **HEAR.**

- Let your baby listen to Daddy or Grandma talking on the other end of the line, and sign **DADDY** or **GRANDMA.**

- As your little one learns to make animal noises or say simple words, you can help him "talk" on the phone by asking him: "What does a **DOG SAY? TELL GRANDMA** what a **DOG SAYS!**" and then have him say it into the phone.

- Play with a toy telephone, signing and talking about people the baby knows.

 DOG, GRANDMA, HEAR, and **LISTEN**

TELEPHONE. The "Y" hand is held to the side of the head like a telephone.

TELL/SAY. The index finger starts at the chin and moves away, representing the flow of words coming out of the mouth.

This activity really only applies to front-loading machines with a window in the door—we call it "Baby TV" at my house. They just can't get enough of watching the water fill and the clothes spin around and around.  If you go to a Laundromat, use this kind of machine; after all, it gets your clothes cleaner *and* keeps your baby entertained!

What to Do

- Turn on the washing machine and sit in front of it with your child. It's easier to sign if you sit next to her, as opposed to holding her on your lap. If she's the restless type or too young to sit or stand, try using a bouncy seat or standing her in her ExerSaucer.

- As you watch the machine fill up, sign **WATER.**

- As the clothes begin swishing around in the suds, sign **WASH.**

- You can also sign **HEAR, SHAKE,** or **LOUD (HEAR + SHAKE = LOUD)** for the spin cycle and the buzzer indicating that the load is finished.

 HEAR and **SHAKE**

Important: Please always use caution with your baby in the laundry area. Keep cleaning products out of reach, check the floor and other surfaces for spilled laundry products, and watch for machine leaks. Also be mindful that items set on top of the machine can fall off when it enters the spin cycle.

WATER. The first 3 fingers form a "W" and tap the chin twice.

WASH. The closed fist scrubs the opposite open palm in a circular motion, as if washing something.

Lights and Ceiling Fans

These are two of baby's favorite things! You can play this game in any room of the house, not to mention in many public places as well.

What to Do

- Simply point to the light or ceiling fan and say and sign **LIGHT** or **FAN.** Do this with great enthusiasm, showing the baby that you appreciate these wonders of modern technology as much as he does!

- Turn the light or fan **ON** and **OFF**, asking the baby if she wants **MORE** in between.

- You can also sign **WIND** when standing near a fan. Tabletop fans often work better for this than the ceiling variety.

 MORE and WIND

LIGHT. The raised hand bends down at the wrist with tips of fingers and thumb held together. The fingers then open, representing rays of light shining down.

Variations: Fingers open mean **LIGHT ON;** fingers closed mean **LIGHT OFF.** Both hands opening and closing repeatedly and quickly mean **FLASHING LIGHTS.**

FAN (CEILING FAN). The index finger is held up, turning around and around, representing the motion of a fan.

Tactile Temperatures

Activities that utilize strong sensory experiences make a huge impression on your baby and are great for helping him learn! Signs like **WET, COLD,** and **WARM** are easy to incorporate into a variety of activities.

What to Do

- Give your baby a cold, water-filled teether to hold and mouth. Sign and say "**COLD.**"

- Sign **COLD** whenever you open the fridge.

- Let your baby learn by touch as you hand her a cold piece of fruit, bottle of milk, or closed juice box, signing **COLD.**

- Put his hand into cold or warm running water or bowls of water. Sign and say "**COLD**" or "**WARM**"; you can also sign **WET** and **WATER.** Try adding some toys to the water!

Important: Always supervise your child closely near water. Let tap water run for a bit and check its temperature with your own hand before putting his fingers under the faucet—it could heat up more than you realize.

- When you're blow-drying your hair, aim the hair dryer in baby's direction (from a safe distance, of course) and sign **WARM.** You can also do this near a heat vent. This is a great time to sign **WIND,** too.

- Fill a toddler's sock with rice, tie a *tight* knot in the end, and heat it for a *short* time in the microwave. Give this to your baby, and sign **WARM** as she handles it.

Important: After heating, please be sure to shake the sock up to spread the heat, and test it on a sensitive part of your skin for a few seconds. It might be hotter than you first think, and your baby's skin is much thinner and more sensitive than yours!

 WATER, WET, and WIND

Continued . . .

COLD. The shoulders
are hunched, and the
clenched hands shake as
if shivering with cold.

WARM. The closed fist
is held close to the
mouth, and then opens
as it moves away,
representing warm
breath coming out.

My son, Aiden, signing COLD.

Loud Noises

Babies can be scared or fascinated by loud noises. Everyday sounds such as the blender, vacuum cleaner, washing machine, or car alarm going off can be startling! Use the sign **LOUD** when these noises occur, or if possible as a warning when they're about to happen. Signing ahead of time will lessen the startling effect, while using the appropriate gesture during the racket—with a reassuring smile on your face—will let your baby know that you hear it, too, and that everything is okay.

My son is fascinated by the volume control on his crib-rail-mounted musical toy and his "soothing sounds" machine (which provides background noise of crickets, ocean waves, running water, birds singing, and the like). He cranks it up all the way and signs **LOUD** over and over.

HEAR + SHAKE = LOUD! The idea here is that the sound is so loud that it shakes the ground.

HEAR. The natural gesture: index finger points to the ear. You may observe your baby doing this naturally in response to sounds, even before you do it.

SHAKE. The two fists move back and forth as if shaking something.

Dance to the Music

Whether it's country, reggae, or
classical, babies love music and dancing. Of course, they also love children's songs, but don't limit yourself
to kids' CDs or it will drive you batty!
This activity is a great way to wear
out your child before a nap.

What to Do

- Before turning on the radio or CD player, ask,
  "Do you want **MUSIC?**" saying and signing
  "**MUSIC,**" and then switch on the stereo.

- Say and sign, "Let's **DANCE** to the **MUSIC!** Can you
  DANCE with Mommy?" Then either let your baby
  dance on her own, or swoop her up in your arms
  and boogie around the living room with her.

- You can also sign **HEAR** or **LOUD.**

 **HEAR** and **LOUD**

MUSIC. The action hand, held on its side, moves rhythmically back and forth over the forearm, which is held in front of the chest.

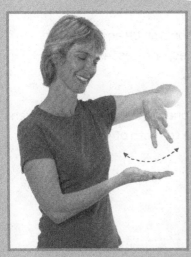

DANCE. The first two fingers of the action hand form an inverted "V" and swing rhythmically back and forth over the upturned palm of the base hand.

Upstairs, Downstairs

If you have stairs in your home, you probably trudge up and down them countless times every day. (At least you're getting a little bit of exercise!) Why not exercise your baby's brain at the same time?

What to Do

- Sign **UP** and **DOWN** just before—and during—ascending and descending the stairs.

- Alternatively, you can sign **UP** and **DOWN** on stairs in public places, or on escalators in department stores.

You may find that **UP** is one of your child's first spoken words—it was the first one for both of my children!

UP. The natural gesture: Index finger points up.

DOWN. The natural gesture: Index finger points down.

47

Clean Up, Clean Up— Everybody, Everywhere!

Whenever you're cleaning or washing anything—mopping the floor, doing the dishes, dusting, vacuuming, or even putting away toys—you can use the opportunity to teach the signs **WASH, DIRTY, CLEAN,** and **HELP.**

Signing is also a great way to help your baby change gears from playtime to cleaning up, which is often difficult for young children. Preschool teachers know this, and they often use special transitional songs to help alert children to a change of activities and carry them smoothly through the transition. See the "Resources" section of this book for songs that you can use at home to ease transitions.

What to Do

- When you're ready to put away toys, tell your baby that it's time to **CLEAN** up, and ask him to **HELP** put toys back on the shelf or into the toy box.

- Sing and sign a cleanup song as you go around the room picking up. Show your child where things go and help him put them away.

While it will be quite a while before your child can clean up all by himself, it's never to early to start teaching him that we put things away when we're finished with them.

 DIRTY and CLEAN

WASH (CLEAN UP). The fist of the action hand scrubs the opposite open palm in a circular motion, as if scrubbing something clean.

Continued . . .

49

HELP. ASL version: The action hand, formed into a fist, is placed on top of the flat base hand. Both rise up together as if the flat hand is helping to lift the fist.

HELP.
Non-ASL version: This is recommended for very young children by Joseph Garcia in *Sign with Your Baby*. Both flat hands pat the chest, which is easier for parents to recognize when done by younger babies.

Aiden and Mommy signing HELP.

Ready to Go

When it's time to go, Mommy grabs a whole bunch of irresistible objects on the way out the door. She takes her **KEYS,** 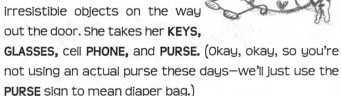 **GLASSES,** cell **PHONE,** and **PURSE.** (Okay, okay, so you're not using an actual purse these days—we'll just use the **PURSE** sign to mean diaper bag.)

What to Do

- When baby hears the jingle of those keys, he knows that it's time to get a move on and will usually look up at you. Take this opportunity to sign **KEYS.**

- You can also sign **PHONE** and **GLASSES** as you stow these in your diaper bag **(PURSE).**

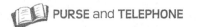 **PURSE** and **TELEPHONE**

KEYS. The index finger of the action hand bends at the knuckle and turns in the sideways palm of the base hand, representing a key turning in a lock.

GLASSES. The thumbs and index fingers indicate the outline of glasses.

Baby's Best Friend

Animal signs are very motivating to babies, and are especially useful if you have pets. Your child spends most of her time at eye level with the family cat or dog, and is eager to share her observations about them!

What to Do

- Sign **CAT** or **DOG** whenever you see your pets lying around or entering a room.

- Comment on what your pets are doing: "**KITTY** is **EATING**" or "**KITTY** is **WASHING** herself."

- If you don't have pets of your own, you can sign about those you see when you visit friends or go for a walk.

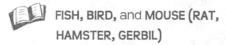 FISH, BIRD, and MOUSE (RAT, HAMSTER, GERBIL)

CAT. The thumb and index finger come together at the upper lip and move outward and away from the face as if sliding whiskers through the fingers. You can use one or both hands.

DOG. The hand pats the knee and/or snaps the fingers, as if calling a dog.

Lights at Night

Whether they're natural or man-made, lights in the dark are fascinating to babies. Try this in your front yard, when camping out, or just looking out the bedroom window!

What to Do

- Hold your baby in your lap and look at the night sky together. Tell him to look **UP** as you point to the sky.

- Point out and sign about the **MOON** and **STARS.**

- If you live near an airport, as I do, you can sign about the **AIRPLANES** with their **FLASHING LIGHTS.**

- If you have a city view, you can indicate the twinkling **LIGHTS** below.

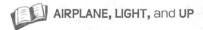 AIRPLANE, LIGHT, and UP

MOON. A modified "C" hand is made with the thumb and forefinger. It taps the temple, then rises up over the head as the signer gazes up at it.

STARS. The two index fingers rub against each other as they point alternately skyward. This represents stars twinkling.

Mirror, Mirror on the Wall

Babies love to look at themselves in the mirror, and they'll often look at you longer in the mirror than they will "in person," which gives you more time to show them signs.

What to Do

- Say "**WHERE** is your nose?" signing **WHERE,** and then circling or pointing to your own nose with your finger. Then exclaim, "There's your nose!" as you point to Baby's nose. Repeat with other body parts.

- Hold up objects (such as a rubber duck, bath book, or toothbrush) and sign their names to Baby in the mirror.

- While looking into the mirror with your child, point to yourself and sign **MOMMY** or **DADDY.** Then point to him and sign **BABY.**

- Point to Baby and sign **BEAUTIFUL** in the mirror. (There are no ugly babies—that's my story and I'm sticking to it!)

📖 BEAUTIFUL, BOOK, DADDY, DUCK, MOMMY, and TOOTHBRUSH

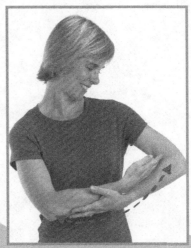

BABY. One arm cradles the other and moves side to side, as if rocking a baby.

WHERE. The hand, index finger extended, waves from side to side describing a small arc, as if you're wondering where something is but just can't put your finger on it.

59

Chapter 5

Signing While Out and About

Most of us don't have the luxury of engaging in all-day playtime with our babies. Even stay-at-home moms still have to make endless trips to the supermarket, post office, bank, and so on.

Fortunately, going anyplace outside of the house can be an adventure for your baby or toddler. Even seemingly mundane errands offer opportunities to explore a new world, and you can sign anytime, anywhere!

Here's another plus: In addition to building your baby's vocabulary, signing about whatever you're doing helps keep fussiness at bay by making him feel a part of what's going on. Even occurrences that seem ordinary and boring to you can be fascinating to him. Use signs everywhere you go in order to help him name all of his new discoveries!

OUT/ OUTSIDE.
For **OUT,** one hand moves out of the other. For **OUTSIDE,** repeat the motion.

GO. Both hands, with index fingers extended, bend at the wrists and point in the direction you're going.

Nature Walk

Whether you're taking a stroller walk around your neighborhood or going on a serious hike in the back-country, you and your baby will find plenty of natural wonders to sign about!

What to Do

- Point out neighborhood pets as you sign **DOG** and **CAT.**

- Stop and smell the flowers, signing **FLOWER, BEAUTIFUL,** and maybe the color.

- Sign **TREE** as you let your baby pat the rough bark or hold her up to grasp the leaves.

- Make the sign for **GRASS** as you run her fingers through the soft blades.

- Point out the birds, signing **BIRD, UP, TREE, HEAR,** and **SING (MUSIC).**

Continued . . .

- Sign **BUTTERFLY** as they flit by, or **BUGS** as they crawl on the ground.

- Show your child the **CLOUDS** and the **SUN** in the sky.

- Indicate the **DUCKS** or **FISH** in the **WATER,** perhaps tossing them some **FOOD.**

- Sign about the **WIND** blowing. Babies love this!

- Point out a cactus garden, signing **PAIN** and **NO TOUCH.** Pretend to touch a cactus, then quickly pull your hand away, exclaiming "Ouch!" and again signing **PAIN.**

BEAUTIFUL, BIRD, BUG, BUTTERFLY, CAT, CLOUDS, DOG, DUCK, FISH, FOOD, GRASS, HEAR, SING (MUSIC), SUN, UP, WATER, and WIND

TREE. The elbow of the action hand rests on the opposite open palm with fingers splayed open ("5" hand) to represent the branches of a tree. The hand pivots back and forth at the wrist.

FLOWER. The fingers and thumb of the action hand are held together, as if holding a tiny blossom by the stem. The hand moves from one side of the nose to the other, as if smelling the flower.

Weather Watching

Changes in the weather offer plenty of opportunities to sign with your baby. Can you imagine how fascinating wind must be to a baby? He must wonder what this invisible thing is that touches his face and ruffles his hair. And what must he think when water suddenly pours from the sky, or when he wakes up and everything is covered in a white blanket of snow?

As adults, we take these natural occurrences for granted—so much so, in fact, that when we say that people were "standing around discussing the weather," we're usually implying that they were making unimportant small talk. To a baby, however, everything is new and exciting. If your child could talk, surely he'd want to discuss the weather!

One day, before I'd ever thought to show my son the sign for **WIND,** he signed "**COMB HAIR**" when he felt the wind on his head. I guess it must have felt to him like the wind was combing his hair! Seeing him do that made me realize that he wanted to be able to talk about the wind, so I taught him the correct sign. Watching for things that interest your child and teaching those signs is the single most effective thing you can do to motivate him!

What to Do

- When you're looking out the window, perhaps when you're deciding what to wear that day, comment on the weather. You might tell your baby that it's **COLD** or **RAINING,** and then show her the appropriate clothes as you take them out.

- If the weather changes when you're out and about, comment on it and sign "Look—it's starting to **RAIN!**" or "The **SUN** came back out! Now it's **WARM** again," or "Look at all the **SNOW!** That's **SNOW,**" or "It's a **WINDY** day. Can you feel the **WIND** in your hair?"

- Go outside and let your baby feel the warm sidewalk; tell her that the **SUN** makes it **WARM.**

- Play outside, even if the weather isn't perfect, signing **RAIN, SNOW, COLD,** and **WET.** For snow, you can also sign **WHITE.**

 COLD, SNOW, SUN, WARM, WET, and WHITE

Continued . . .

RAIN. The hands are held palms down with fingers spread and bent. They make a double downward movement, representing rain falling.

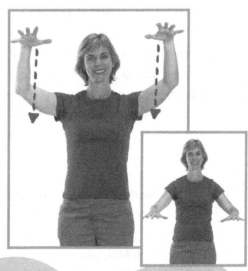

WIND. Both open hands are held sideways in front of the body. The hands sway gracefully from side to side like trees blowing in the wind.

68

At the Playground

The playground offers plenty of
opportunities to play and sign, while
combining the lessons with physical
actions and sensations. Signing **UP**
when your baby is at the top of the
slide, for example (and then signing **DOWN** as he slides
to the bottom), helps him make a very clear connection
between the gesture and its real-life meaning. This is
signing in context at its best!

What to Do

- Ask your baby if she'd like to **SWING**. Put her in
  a baby swing and give her a push, saying and
  signing "**SWING**" as she moves back and forth.
  Every now and then, stop the ride and sign **STOP**.
  Then ask her, "Do you want **MORE?**" After a brief
  pause, begin pushing the swing again.

- Ask your baby if he'd like to **SLIDE**. If he's too
  little to go by himself, you can hold him as you
  slide him down. Then ask him if he'd like to go

Continued ...

AGAIN or **MORE.** (This is also a great opportunity to sign **UP, DOWN,** and **GO.**)

- As your toddler climbs on play structures, sign **UP** and **DOWN.**

- When your baby tries to eat dirt, sand, and sticks, say and sign "**NO,**" "**EAT,**" and "**DIRTY**" while making a "yucky face" and blowing "raspberries" with your tongue.

- Sometimes playground equipment can get **HOT, WARM,** or **COLD.** Test these sensations with your baby and sign about them.

 AGAIN, COLD, DIRTY, DOWN, EAT, HOT, GO, MORE, NO, STOP, UP, and WARM

SWING. The first two fingers of the action hand (held in a "V"), "sit" on the first two fingers of the base hand, which are held together to represent the seat of a swing. Swing the hands together.

SLIDE. The first two fingers of the action hand are held in a "V" shape, representing legs. They slide down the first two fingers of the opposite hand, which are held together, representing a playground slide.

Car Ride

Most babies love to ride in the car. Once your child is old enough to face forward in her car seat, you'll have loads of fun signing about all the things you see! You might even start looking forward to waiting at a train crossing, because you'll be able to sign **TRAIN, LOUD,** and **LIGHTS!**

What to Do

- When it's time to go, say, "It's time to go for a ride in the **CAR!**"

- Most babies get to a stage sometime after one year of age where they want to get into their car seat and clip the harness themselves. Tell your child that you'll **HELP** with this, and then give him a hand. You can also sign for him to get **IN, OUT, UP,** or **DOWN** or to **SIT.**

- Babies often like to look at and play with the overhead light in the car. You can turn the switch off and on and sign **LIGHT.**

- When you're stuck in traffic, sign about **CARS** or that a nearby bus or truck is **BIG.**

- Sign **STOP** when you pull up to a red light (or stop sign) and **GO** when the light turns green. You can also sign about the colors of the lights.

 BIG, BUS, DOWN, FIRE TRUCK, GO, IN, LIGHT, LOUD, OUT, STOP, UP, TRAIN, and TRUCK

CAR. The two fists mimic the steering of a car. For **TRUCK** or **BUS,** steer a wheel that's bigger and lower down (see the "Signing Vocabulary" section).

SIT. The first two fingers of the action hand form a "V" and then bend at the knuckles to "sit" on the first two fingers of the base hand.

Supermarket Signing

A trip to the market with an infant or toddler in tow is often an occasion for dread. It can be a crapshoot as to whether or not you'll actually make it home with groceries, or if your baby will have a complete meltdown or diaper blowout midway through the outing, forcing you to leave your half-filled cart at the store. I'm afraid that I can't help you out with the diaper-blowout scenario, but I can offer a few suggestions on how to keep shopping-cart fussiness at bay—with signing!

The primary reason babies get fussy at the store is that they aren't getting much attention from Mom or Dad. The adults are focusing on grocery lists, coupons, and ingredient labels, and the baby is getting b-o-r-e-d.

This doesn't need to be the case, however—in fact, the supermarket has the potential to be a pretty entertaining place for a baby. There are shelves upon shelves of things to see and sign about. The trick is to help your child feel a little more involved in what's going on, and signing is a great way to do that.

What to Do

- Play and sign **STOP** and **GO** as you push baby in the cart.

- Show and sign about different fruits and vegetables in the produce section.

- Practice using any food signs you know when you encounter those items on the shelves.

- Sign about pictures on labels, bags, or boxes.

- Use animal signs when pointing out pictures of **CATS, DOGS, MICE** (which can be used for any small rodents), and **BIRDS** on packages in the pet-supplies section.

- Your baby is bound to get hungry signing about all of the food, so keep some snacks on hand. (More than once, I've had to break open a box of cookies or crackers that I had to pay for later!) You can sign **EAT** and **MORE** as you dole out snacks to your baby in the cart.

Continued . . .

APPLE, BANANA, BIRD, CAT, COOKIE, CRACKER, DOG, FRUIT, GO, MOUSE, ORANGE, STOP, and **VEGETABLE**

STORE/SELL. The fingers and thumbs are held together, making the "flat 0" hand shape. They point to the body, then move outwards at the wrists. This represents holding up something that you're selling.

If you do the wrist motion only once it means **SELL;** repeated multiple times, it means **STORE.** When signing with hearing babies, we tend to repeat motions a lot anyway (to ensure that the babies see our sign), but it's good to know this difference for your own information.

EAT/FOOD. The fingers and thumb, held together as if grasping a small piece of food, tap the mouth several times.

Chapter 6

Signing with Toys

S igning along while you and your baby play is a lot of fun. You don't need to purchase any special toys, since you probably already own plenty that are perfect for signing. For example, you can sign along with stuffed or model animals, dolls, busy boxes, balls, rattles, little cars, toy telephones, keys, and musical instruments, just to name a few.

These signs will get you started on your playtime adventures:

FUN, FUNNY, and SILLY

TOY. Make two fists with your thumbs between your first two fingers; these are "T" hands. Shake your "T" hands.

PLAY. Raise the thumbs and pinkies of both hands to form a "Y" hand shape. Shake hands, pivoting at the wrists, representing the shaking of a tambourine.

Give and Take

The first time I saw a baby signing **PLEASE** for something, I was totally blown away. How could a little ten-month-old possibly understand the concept of manners? Well, the truth is that children that age actually can't understand the concept of manners yet—and won't until they're at least three years old.

What babies *can* do, however, is learn that they need to sign **PLEASE** first if they want something. This is similar to teaching toddlers to "Use your magic words." First they say them "just because," and then later they learn to use them because it's nice manners.

Playing one-on-one with your baby is a great time to work on manners signs and signs such as **GIVE** and **GIVE ME.** When you're using signs with toys that Baby especially likes or things that are new and interesting to her, she's bound to do a lot of reaching for what you're holding. Do this activity at home or use the contents of your purse to keep her entertained while you're waiting for an appointment at the doctor's office.

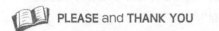 **PLEASE** and **THANK YOU**

Continued . . .

What to Do

Signing **PLEASE:**

- Pick up a toy or an object from your purse and show interest in it.

- When your baby reaches for the object, tell him, "Sign **PLEASE**" while making the gesture yourself. Then reach over and sign it on your baby's chest, using his hand or your own.

- Now give your baby the toy or object. It will probably be a while before he actually does produce the right movements, so don't try to withhold the object until he does so.

Signing **GIVE** and **GIVE ME:**

- As you play with your baby, ask her to give you things as you sign **GIVE ME.** You can also do this when she's picked up something she shouldn't have: "**GIVE** Mommy the letter opener, sweetie. That's a good girl."

- When she gives you the object, say and sign, **THANK YOU!**"

- Now and then, ask your baby, "Do you want me to **GIVE** you this (toy, doll, car, blanket)?"

- Wait for her to respond by smiling, reaching, or—if you're lucky—*signing,* and then hand the object to her, reminding her to say "**THANK YOU!**"

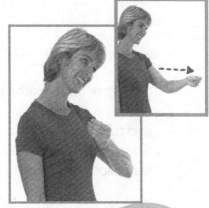

GIVE. The thumb and fingers are held together as if grasping something, and the hand moves away from the signer as if giving something away. You can use one or both hands.

GIVE ME. The thumb and fingers are held together as if grasping something. The hand starts a distance away from the body, and then moves in closer, as if taking something from someone.

83

Rattle Play

Rattles are, of course, one of Baby's very first toys. Because these toys make a noise, they're especially effective for getting your child's attention as you sign.

What to Do

- Show your baby a rattle and sign **RATTLE.**

- Hold the rattle near your face and in his field of vision, giving it a few shakes. Ask him: "Do you want **MORE?**" or "Do you want **MORE RATTLE?**"

- Shake the rattle again. Repeat several times.

RATTLE. The hand mimics shaking a rattle.

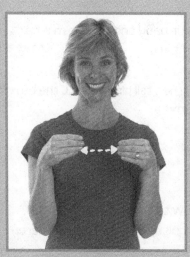

MORE. The thumbs and fingertips of each hand are held together, and the fingertips of both hands tap together several times. This represents gathering more things together.

85

Your baby loves it when you take the time to play with her and will be delighted by even the simplest of games. Most children enjoy playing with a ball, and **BALL** is an easy sign for them to learn, too. In the beginning, they'll probably approximate this sign by clapping hands.

What to Do

Roll the Ball (A medium to large ball that rolls well works best for this game.):

- Sit across from your baby and show him a ball, saying and signing "**BALL**."

- Roll the ball to him, then tell him to **ROLL** the ball to **MOMMY** (or **DADDY**).

Throw the Ball:

- Show your baby how to throw. (A smallish ball, especially a soft, squishy one, works best here.)

- Give the ball to her and tell her to throw it, signing **THROW**.

- Try using a laundry basket or large bin for a "basketball" variation on this game.

 DADDY, MOMMY, and **THROW**

BALL. The curved hands, with fingers spread, bounce toward each other, as if holding a ball.

ROLL. The index fingers roll over one another as they move forward.

Pretend Shopping

My daughter invented this game, which she called "Buy New," when she was just a toddler. It's great for practicing all the toy signs you know, as well as many others.

You'll need two shopping bags and various toys and other items that you know signs for.

What to Do

- Line up all your items on the floor or on a low table. These are "for sale."

- Pretend to come into the "store" with your child, each carrying a bag.

- Choose items and put them into your bags, signing about each one as you do so.

- After the "shopping" part is done, you can sit together and barter between your two bags. Sign about items as you take them **IN** and **OUT**. For example, you might say: "I'll give you this

BUNNY, if you give me a **CAR,**" and then tell him,
Put the **BUNNY IN** your bag."

Older toddlers will enjoy making the game more
elaborate:

- You can pretend to get into an imaginary **CAR**
  and drive to the store.

- **OPEN** and **CLOSE** a pretend door as you go in.

- When it's time to check out, have one person
  pretend to be the cashier, scanning items,
  taking money, and giving change.

- Sign that you're **FINISHED** shopping and pretend
  to drive home.

 CAR, FINISHED, IN, OPEN, RABBIT (BUNNY),
STORE, and WANT

Continued . . .

IN. One hand pretends to put something in the other.

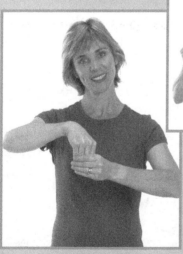

OUT/ OUTSIDE. For **OUT,** one hand moves out of the other. For **OUTSIDE,** repeat the motion.

Dolly Play

Ask any parent which signs they feel are the most important ones for their baby to learn, and you'll probably find that **EAT, DIAPER CHANGE, MORE,** and **MILK** are pretty high on the list. However, because babies are already in the habit of crying for these things, it may take a while for them to realize that there's a better way.

Playing and signing with dolls introduces these routine signs in a playful context, getting your baby's attention and motivating her to sign more herself!

What to Do

- At play- or mealtime, pretend to feed a doll or stuffed animal and sign **EAT.**

- Let your baby help put one of his diapers on a doll or stuffed animal and sign **CHANGE, DIAPER, WET, POOP,** and **CLEAN** as you talk about what you're doing.

Continued . . .

- If you're potty training, try putting the doll on the seat. Sign **POTTY (TOILET), POOP, WIPE (WASH),** and **FINISHED.** Praise dolly lavishly for being such a big girl (or boy)!

- Give a doll or stuffed animal a drink from a toy bottle or your baby's bottle, or pretend to nurse it, signing **MILK, WATER, JUICE,** or **DRINK.**

- Give dolly a pretend bath in a basin, or put her in the tub with your child. Sign **BATH, WASH, WET, SHAMPOO, DIRTY, CLEAN, DRY,** and **TOWEL.** You can also sign about body parts!

- Ask your baby to **HELP** dolls do difficult things, such as getting onto a baby bike or climbing up onto the couch. Sign **HELP, UP,** and **DOWN.**

- Play "doctor" or "vet" with a doll or stuffed animal, putting on bandages and signing **PAIN** or doing an exam with a toy doctor's kit. This is a great one to familiarize and help put your child at ease about doctor visits.

 CLEAN, DIAPER, DIRTY, DOWN, DRINK, DRY, EAT, FINISHED, HELP, JUICE, PAIN, POOP, SHAMPOO, TOILET, TOWEL, UP, WASH, WATER, and WET

MILK. The sideways-held fist is opened and closed several times, as if milking a cow.

CHANGE. The two fists are held together, facing opposite directions, with knuckles touching. Both hand pivot in opposite directions, to change places.

Animal Toys

Animals are probably the single most prolific theme in baby toys. Just take a look at your own household's toy chest: You'll find animal rattles and puppets, stuffed animals, pop-up animals, and toys that make animal noises—and probably many more! This theme is clearly a big favorite with babies and toddlers.

Because of this, you'll have plenty of opportunities to teach these signs, even if you never set foot in a barnyard or zoo. When you practice these gestures with your baby, be sure to make animal noises and faces, too!

What to Do

- Sign along with toys that have animal pictures and sounds, such as a See 'n Say.

- Play with animal puppets as you sign with your other hand.

- Have fun with a toy farm or zoo and its plastic inhabitants.

- Sign about animals that pop out of a busy box or jack-in-the-box.

- Hide a stuffed animal under a blanket and play "**WHERE** is the animal?"

- Shake an animal rattle at your baby as you sign the creature's name and **RATTLE.**

- Let your baby chew on cold, animal-shaped teethers, signing **COLD** and the animal's name.

- Sign about the critters on your baby's mobile, wallpaper, or other room decor.

- Play with plastic animals in a basin of water or the tub using animal and bath signs.

- Play outside with plastic animals in a sandbox or on the grass.

Continued . . .

ALLIGATOR, BEAR, BIRD, CAT, COLD, COW, DOG, DUCK, ELEPHANT, FISH, FROG, HIPPOPOTOMUS, GIRAFFE, LION, MONKEY, MOUSE, RABBIT, RATTLE, SHEEP, SNAKE, TIGER, and WHERE

ANIMAL. The fingertips rest lightly on the chest as the backs of the hands move toward and away from each other repeatedly. This represents the rise and fall of an animal's chest as it breathes.

BEAR. Both hands form "claws" that cross the chest and make scratching motions, like a bear scratching itself.

My niece Ruby signs KITTY.

Trains, Planes, and Automobiles

Both boys and girls are very  interested in "things that go." When you take a walk, your baby is likely to spend a lot of time pointing and commenting, "Ohhh!" and Uhhh!" at cars, trucks, buses, airplanes, bicycles, and helicopters. Adding a few age-appropriate toy vehicles to your baby's collection provides plenty of opportunity to use these signs at home as well.

What to Do

- Play with a toy school bus and dolls , signing **BUS, STOP, GO, IN,** and **OUT.**

- Have fun with a toy airplane or helicopter, signing **UP, DOWN, AIRPLANE,** and **HELICOPTER.** Remember to make appropriate noises as you make them fly!

- Race a toy car across the floor or lean a board against a chair for a ramp to race down, signing **CAR, UP, DOWN, GO, STOP.**

- Play with toys that your child can ride on, signing **STOP, GO, BIKE,** or **CAR** as appropriate.

- Sail a toy **BOAT** in the tub, an outdoor water table, or large dishpan of water.

  Important: Always supervise your baby closely around water, even if it's just a dishpan!

- Play with toy trains (with or without tracks), signing **TRAIN, STOP,** and **GO.**

- Make a toy **TRACTOR** or **TRUCK** go "Vroom!" in the sandbox or on the beach.

BIKE, BUS, BOAT, DOWN, GO, HELICOPTER, IN, OUT, STOP, TRACTOR, TRAIN, TRUCK, and UP

Continued . . .

AIRPLANE. The "Y" hand, with index finger extended and palm down, moves up and away from the body, representing the wings and fuselage of an airplane flying through the sky.

CAR. Both hands move in opposite arc motions while grasping an imaginary steering wheel.

Shape Sorters and Puzzles

Shape sorters and puzzles are great for toddlers' hand-eye coordination and small-motor development. Try fun shape sorters that make a noise when your baby gets the piece in the right hole and wooden puzzles that have a corresponding picture in the space where the piece goes.

In the beginning, your child will need help doing these activities. This is the perfect time to use the sign for **HELP,** as you assist him.

What to Do

- Show your baby the puzzle or shape sorter.

- Take a piece and tell her that you're going to put it **IN,** then do so and sign **IN** again.

- Now give her a piece (if she hasn't already picked one up), and tell *her* to put it **IN.**

Continued . . .

- If she has trouble ask and sign, "Do you need **HELP?** Mommy will **HELP** you." Then put a piece partway in and tell or help her to push it the rest of the way.

- If your baby takes pieces out, say and sign, "You took that one **OUT.**"

- Be sure to praise her lavishly when she puts pieces in, takes them out, or attempts to sign, even if you had to help her. Say and sign, "**HOORAY!**"—for both of you!

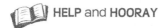 HELP and HOORAY

IN. One hand moves into the other.

OUT/ OUTSIDE. For **OUT,** one hand moves out of the other. For **OUTSIDE,** repeat the motion.

Dressing Up

Even the youngest toddlers love to dress up, whether in your clothes or special outfits. My mother finds old Halloween costumes and kids' sequined dance outfits at thrift stores for only pennies—and she finds so many that I've had to tell her to stop buying them!

The smaller the baby, the simpler the props need to be. A 10- to 16-month-old will be fine with hats or scarves, for example, because things that are difficult for them to pull off by themselves are frustrating to very little ones. Older toddlers will enjoy putting on Mommy's shoes and dresses, or Daddy's shirts and ties.

Use clothing signs, as well as descriptive signs such as **ON, OFF, BIG, LITTLE,** and **BEAUTIFUL.**

What to Do

- Lay some dress-up clothes on the floor and then sit across from your baby.

- Put on a hat, or other item of clothing, and then say and sign, "Mommy has a **HAT** (or whatever)! Mommy put the **HAT ON!**"

- Let your child take the hat off your head, and say and sign, "You took the **HAT OFF!**"

- Try putting the item on your baby, signing that it's **ON** or **OFF**, or that she looks **BEAUTIFUL** in it.

- If you're playing with dresses or scarves, this is a great time to **DANCE!** Put on some music beforehand so that you'll be ready to twirl in your dresses, sway in your hula skirts, or swirl your scarves.

 BEAUTIFUL, BIG, DANCE, HAT, and LITTLE

ON. One hand lies on top of the other, palm down.

OFF. One hand moves off of the other.

Making Music

Every night after dinner, we try to make time to play together as a family. One of our favorite things is to put on some boisterous sea chantys or marching music and parade around the living room playing maracas, tambourines, drums, and jingle bells. (Fortunately, our neighbors aren't too close!) Maybe when the kids are bigger, this will give way to board games, but for now, it's something that even our 14-month-old can participate in.

You can buy children's instruments or simply make your own by filling small plastic containers with beans, rice, or gravel.

What to Do

- Put on some fun marching-type music, and sign **MUSIC!**

- March around the room playing your instruments with great enthusiasm.

- In between songs, sign **HOORAY** and **MORE!**

- Sing and twirl as you go, signing **DANCE!**

DANCE, LOUD, and HOORAY!

MUSIC. The action hand, held on its side, moves rhythmically back and forth over the forearm, which is held in front of the chest.

MORE. The thumbs and fingertips of each hand are held together, while the fingertips of both hands tap together several times. This represents gathering more things together.

Blocks and Building Toys

Toddlers enjoy stacking these toys, knocking them down, and putting them in  and taking them out of containers. Traditional wooden blocks or large interlocking Lego-type blocks are great for toddlers. While there's no recognized ASL sign for "blocks," there are plenty of others that you can use while playing with them. (Make sure that any toys you use are too large to fit through a toilet-paper roll!)

What to Do

- Show your baby the blocks and demonstrate how to stack one on top of another, saying and signing "**BUILD.**"

- Add more blocks to your structure, saying and signing "**MORE**" or "**MORE BUILD.**"

- Encourage your child to participate in **BUILDING;** ask if she wants **HELP.**

- Sign about the color and size of individual blocks,

and about what you build: "Emma made a **BIG HOUSE!**" or "Mommy made a **LITTLE HOUSE!**"

- When she knocks the blocks down (you may never get beyond stacking two or three), say and sign "**FALL DOWN!**"

 BIG, HELP, HOUSE, LITTLE, and MORE

BUILD. The hands show things being stacked on top of each other.

FALL DOWN. The first two fingers make an upside-down "V" on the opposite hand, representing a person standing. Then they "fall" off the hand.

109

Cardboard Boxes

We've all heard it before: "The kid's favorite toy was the box it came in!" Cardboard containers of all sizes can be used in different ways, so don't throw them away— save them for some fun on a rainy day!

What to Do

- Stack small boxes like blocks, signing **BUILD** and **FALL DOWN.**

- Make beds for dolls and stuffed animals from shoe boxes and sign **SLEEP (BED).**

- Cut out windows and doors on large appliance boxes and decorate the structure with pens or crayons to make houses, boats, or submarines. Sign **BOAT, HOUSE, HIDE, IN,** and **OUT.**

- Make a puppet theater from a large appliance box and sign along with puppets. Just stand it on end, cut out the back, and cut a window higher up in the front—and voilà, instant puppet theater! You can also use this for a lemonade stand, or a pretend drive-through window.

 BED, BOAT, BUILD, FALL DOWN, HIDE, HOUSE, and SLEEP

IN. One hand moves into the other.

OUT/ OUTSIDE. For OUT, one hand moves out of the other. For OUTSIDE, repeat the motion.

111

Signing and Colors

When I was signing with my first child, Sirena, I never bothered to teach her color signs. For some reason I thought that the concepts would be too abstract. But after I had my second child, I bought a set of signing board books by Kim Votry (see the "Resources" section), which included a book of color signs. When my son handed it to me at story time one day, little did I know that I was about to be amazed at how motivating color signs can be.

Wow! This book instantly became his favorite. Not only did he learn all the signs right away, but he also started pointing things out and signing their colors! One day we were out for a walk, and at a corner, we came to a wheelchair ramp that had a large, bright yellow, bumpy plate on it. My son stopped to feel the bumps and oohed and ahhhed about this new thing in his world. Then his little hand went up, rotating back and forth at the wrist, approximating the sign for **YELLOW.**

At that moment I suddenly understood how important these signs can be to a child. Color may be the only way a child has of commenting on or describing an unfamiliar object. My son had no idea what this thing was. He didn't know the signs for **BUMPY, RECTANGLE,** or anything else that he might have been able to say about it—except that it was very, very **YELLOW!**

Soon after that, he signed **BLACK TREES** to describe silhouettes of trees at night, and **PINK BIRDS** to tell Grandma about the flamingos at the zoo.

Learning color signs will vastly improved your baby's ability to communicate his or her thoughts and observations. He can even tell you which balloon he wants at the supermarket!

Color Activities

- Read a color book together and sign about each color, or just sign about the colors of the illustrations in any ordinary picture book.

- Sign toy colors: A **RED** truck, **BLUE** car, **GREEN** ball, or **YELLOW** rattle.

- Describe things by color: Sign **BLUE** as you look up at the sky together. Show your baby leaves and tell him that they're **GREEN** or that flowers are **PINK.** Point out the big **YELLOW** bulldozer digging up the road, and tell him to hold your hand to cross the **BLACK** street. Show him that snow is **WHITE** and **COLD!**

Continued . . .

- Sign the colors of cars or trucks when you're driving or out for a walk.

- Let your child choose things by color, such as which balloon he'd like, which shirt to wear, and which crayon or finger paint to use.

The list goes on and on—if you can sign colors, you can sign all day long!

BLUE. Make a "B" hand shape by holding up your flat hand with your fingers together and your thumb bent inward across your palm. Shake your "B" in the space off the right shoulder. (This is the area where some color signs are made.)

GREEN. Make a "G" hand shape by holding your hand sideways with your thumb and forefinger almost touching, as if you're about to pinch something. Shake the "G" hand in the space off the right shoulder. (This is the area where some color signs are made.)

RED. The index finger points to the lips, then moves downwards, indicating the red color of the lips.

YELLOW. Make a "Y" hand by raising only your thumb and pinkie. Shake the "Y" hand to the right, in the space off your right shoulder. (This is the area where some color signs are made.)

115

Chapter 7

Active Signing Games

Besides being educational, signing can add extra excitement to more active playtime. You can play typical children's games or make up your own. This isn't limited to preverbal babies, either—older toddlers, preschoolers, and even young grade-school children love to play active signing games. Try these at home, at school, or at the park.

Rolling, Rolling, Rolling! Keep Them Babies Rolling!

This is a simple game that will delight children over six months of age. Play it on any soft surface, such as a carpet, a bed, or a blanket on the lawn.

What to Do

- Say and sign to your baby "Do you want to **ROLL?** It's time to **ROLL** the baby!"

- With both hands, carefully roll him, being careful to support his head and neck (if he's younger). You can chant, "Rolling, rolling, here we go rolling!" in a singsong voice, if you like.

- Stop rolling and ask, "Do you want **MORE?** Do you want **MORE ROLLING?**"

- Gently roll the baby again.

ROLL. The index fingers roll over one another as they move forward.

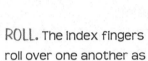

MORE. The thumbs and fingertips of each hand are held together, and the fingertips of both hands tap together several times. This represents gathering more things together.

119

Do It Again—I Want More!

Babies love physically active games, as do parents. Daddies, especially, enjoy flying their infants around like airplanes, bouncing toddlers up in the air, and running around the yard. Signing with these activities is natural, since playing games that are fun and exciting motivates kids to ask for **MORE** and **AGAIN, AGAIN!**

What to Do

- Ask your baby if she'd like to play **AIRPLANE.** Then pick her up, supporting her with one arm under her chest and the other between her legs, with your forearm supporting her hips and tummy. Swing her around in a circle, and then put her down and ask if she wants **MORE.**

- Chase your toddler around the house or yard on your hands and knees, pretending to be an animal. Stop now and then and ask if he wants **MORE BEAR, LION, DOGGY,** and so on.

- Put the baby in a front carrier and chase your older child or spouse around the yard, while roaring. After you catch whomever you're chasing, ask the baby if she wants **MORE,** or if she wants to play **AGAIN.** Take a turn being chased, too. If you're playing with an older sibling, encourage the big brother or sister to sign to the little one.

- Bounce your toddler up over your head a couple of times, then put him down and ask if he wants **MORE.** Repeat until your arms feel as if they're going to fall off!

- Drag your baby around the house or yard on an old blanket or towel, stopping from time to time to ask if she wants **MORE.**

Important: Rough, bouncy games shouldn't be played with new babies. The livelier activities should wait until after 12 months, when the child's neck muscles are stronger. Always play over a soft surface, such as grass or carpet, and use common sense: Don't run too fast, or in places where you could trip over something.

Continued . . .

AGAIN. The fingertips of the curved action hand come down in an arc to touch the upturned palm of the base hand.

MORE. The thumbs and fingertips of each hand are held together, and the fingertips of both hands tap together several times. This represents gathering more things together.

Stop and Go
(Red Light, Green Light)

In this game, the leader acts as the "traffic light," and the other players do what the leader signs and says. Depending on how old your baby is, he can be carried, "walked" while holding on to a parent's hands, or walk on his own. You can also play this with toddlers on riding toys.

This game is great for teaching the concepts of **STOP** and **GO.** When we do this in my classes, all of the children start laughing hysterically every time the parents holding them come to an abrupt stop. It really gets the point across!

What to Do

- The leader stands facing the players, some distance away from them, and then says and signs "**GO!**"

- Players run, walk, or crawl forward.

- The leader says and signs "**STOP!**" and everyone halts abruptly.

- Repeat until all of the players reach the leader, then change leaders and play again. Continued . . .

123

STOP. The edge of one hand comes down on the palm of the other, representing something coming to an abrupt stop.

GO. Both hands, with the index fingers extended, bend at the wrists and point in the direction you're going.

Simon Says

This is an especially fun game for
toddlers, preschoolers, and even older
children. You can do all kinds of silly
things—there's practically no limit to the
signs you can use for actions, animals, or whatever else
you can dream up!

What to Do

- The players stand in a horizontal line, facing the
  leader (Simon), who declares, "Simon says" and
  then speaks and signs the word for an action,
  animal, or thing.

- Everyone acts out the sign.

- They continue to perform the sign until the
  leader tells them: "Simon says **STOP!**"

Example: "Simon says **JUMP!**" Players begin jumping.
"Simon says **STOP JUMPING!**" Everybody stops moving.

Continued . . .

DANCE like a ballerina; drive a **CAR; WASH** the dishes; and bark like a **DOG.**

JUMP. The first two fingers of the action hand form an inverted "V" on the palm of the base hand. The action hand springs up and down, representing legs jumping.

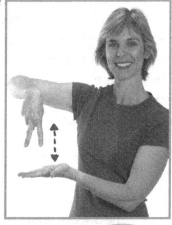

ELEPHANT. Starting at the nose, the "C" hand traces the shape of an elephant's trunk.

My niece Ruby (right) signs JUMP to her sister, Rachel.

Signing Charades

Many parents would like their children to remember signs even after they begin talking. A great way to encourage this is to play signing games occasionally. This is a really fun one for your signing toddler or preschooler that will reinforce their signs.

There are two ways that you can play this—either using strictly signs, or mixing some signs and some mime. Either way, you're in for a really hilarious time!

What to Do

In both versions of this game, one player gets to be the signer and the other player(s) guess what's being signed.

- **Version 1:** The signer makes the gestures for various objects as the other players try to guess what the signs are.

   Example: Sign **BIRD** or **CAR** without saying the words that you're signing.

- **Version 2:** The signer makes the gestures for various situations or concepts, as the other players try to guess them. First sign the concept, and then act it out using signs and pantomime.

Example: For giving the **DOG** a **BATH,** the signer makes the movements for **DOG** and **BATH,** and then mimes walking into a room, turning on a faucet, and signing **WATER.** Then the signer pats leg to call a **DOG** (this is the sign for **DOG**) and mimes putting the dog into a tub and washing it, signing **BATH.** Other signs that could be used are **WASH, SOAP, DIRTY,** and **CLEAN.**

 BATH, BIRD, CAR, DOG, SOAP, and WATER

CLEAN. One flat palm wipes dirt off the other flat palm.

DIRTY. Hold hand under chin and wiggle fingers. (You're in dirt up to your neck!)

Hide and Seek

You can play this game with a toddler and both parents, or with a group of children. When playing with toddlers, an adult should help the children "hide" and "seek" (making sure that they stay safe).

What to Do

- Help the "seeker" child hide her face and count, while the other player (a parent, friend, or sibling) hides.

- When counting time is finished, sign and say, "**WHERE** is **DADDY/ MOMMY?**"

- Help the "seeker" look for the "hider." Build up the fun and suspense by looking in all kinds of funny places, such as under rugs and in little drawers.

 **MOMMY** and **DADDY**

WHERE. The hand, with index finger extended, waves from side to side in a small arc.

HIDE. The thumbnail of the "A" hand touches the chin, then swoops down to hide under the opposite downturned palm.

131

Freeze Dance

Here's one to wear out the children and get them ready for a long nap! Like our "Red Light, Green Light" game, this game is great for teaching the concepts of stop and go.

What You'll Need

- CD or cassette player
- Fun, fast music
- *Optional:* colored scarves to wave around

What to Do

- Have an adult operate the CD or cassette player.

- Turn on the music and say and sign "**GO!**" Toddlers can dance on their own; babies can be held by an adult who dances.

- Have everyone dance their hearts out for a short time, then shut off the music and say "Stop!" or "Freeze!" as you sign **STOP.**

- Keep repeating this until everyone's exhausted; then sign **FINISHED.**

- You can also use the sign for **DANCE** with this game, instead of **GO**.

STOP. The edge of one hand comes down on the palm of the other, representing something coming to an abrupt stop.

GO. Both hands, with the index fingers extended, bend at the wrists and point in the direction you're going.

Peekaboo

This is a fun one that we came up with when my husband was out working in the garden, and the kids and I were inside, sitting around the kitchen table.

What to Do

- Hold your baby or put him in a high chair, facing a window.

- Have Daddy (or someone else) go outside, sneak around to the window, and then pop up. Say and sign, "There's **DADDY!**"

- Daddy crouches down out of sight again. Ask and sign "**WHERE'S DADDY?**"

- Daddy pops up once more!

- Repeat until Daddy thinks he's going to drop from exhaustion.

WHERE. The hand, with index finger extended, waves from side to side in a small arc.

135

Chapter 8

Thinking and Memory Games

As babies increase their signing vocabulary, they often enjoy naming all the things that they know signs for. When your child reaches this stage, it can be fun to make a game of signing the correct names for things. Remember that these should be games—not pop quizzes! Don't pressure your baby to perform for others, finish the game, or try harder. Play only as long as she appears to be enjoying the activity, and definitely stop if either one of you begins to lose interest or get frustrated.

Remember that every baby is different. Some love to demonstrate all they know, are eager to please, and

My daugter, Sirena, at age one, signing SQUIRREL with me.

will often sign when prompted. This is great for taking pictures of them showing off for their grandparents.

Then there are the babies who will sign only when *they* feel like it. If you have one of these, you might feel like nobody believes that she actually uses signs! For example, maybe she won't do a thing when you ask, "What's the sign for **DOG?**" but the next minute she'll hear barking outside and start signing **DOG** like crazy! With this type of child, be especially careful not to turn signing games into a drill session.

I've been blessed with one of each type of signing baby: My daughter, Sirena, is the eager-to-please one; and my son, Aiden, is the one who does it on his own terms. Both have turned out to be amazing signers, each with their own individual style and personality.

Name That Thing

This idea was contributed by signing teacher Brandy Brass-Rafeek, owner of Sweet Signs in Barrie, Ontario, Canada. (If you live near Barrie, you can get information about local classes at **www.sweetsigns .ca**.) Brandy says that this is a fun thing to do when your baby is alert, but not involved in any particular activity.

What to Do

- Ask your baby "**WHERE** is **DADDY?**" or **WHERE** is the **BALL?**"

- When he points correctly, praise him and show him how proud you are that he got it right.

- Start with things that are very familiar to baby and gradually increase the challenge. After a while, try introducing various adjectives along with the nouns. For example, you can ask, "Where is the **BIG BALL?**" or "Where is the **BLUE CAR?**"

- You can also play this game with the sign for **WHAT:** You could hold up your hairbrush and say and sign "**WHAT** is this?"

- Wait for a response, but whether or not you get one, go ahead and say and sign, "That's right—it's Mommy's **BRUSH.**"

 BALL, BLUE, BRUSH, CAR, and DADDY

WHERE. The hand, with index finger extended, waves from side to side in a small arc.

WHAT. The hands are raised, palms up, in the natural "What?" gesture.

141

Match the Sign

This game was invented by Jamie Anderson of Fort Wayne, Indiana. She signs with all four of her children, ages two, three, four, and seven.

You'll use flash cards with pictures or images cut from magazines (it's a good idea to "laminate" them with clear contact paper if you want to use them more than once!)

What to Do

- Lay out pictures of things that your child knows signs for.

- Make one of the signs to her and have her find the matching picture.

- When you find a match, say "**HOORAY!**" while raising your hands into the air and shaking them. This is the ASL version of applause.

- *Alternate version:* You point to the picture and have your child make the sign for it.

HOORAY! (This is also the sign for **YIPPEE, YAHOO,** and **YEAH.**) Raise both open hands up in the air and shake them as you cheer.

The whole point of clapping your hands is to make the loud noise—which you wouldn't hear anyway if you were deaf. Hence, the raised-hands-shaking sign for **HOORAY!**

SIGNO
(ASL version of BINGO)

This is my version of a game that I first heard about from Nancy Hanauer, owner of Signing with Your Baby in Seattle, Washington. (For information on Nancy's classes, go to **www.signingbabies.net**.)

SIGNO is most appropriate for preschool and school-age kids, and maybe some older toddlers. It's a great way to help children and parents remember their signs and practice their receptive skills (recognizing a sign when it's signed *to* you). If you get together with other parents who sign with their babies, this is a fun activity to do together.

What You'll Need

- SIGNO cards (see instructions in Chapter 10)

- "Draw" cards (see instructions in Chapter 10)

- Washable crayons (Crayola makes some) or pieces of cereal to mark off the spaces

What to Do

- Decide who will be the signer and give each of the remaining players a SIGNO card.

- Put draw cards into a hat, basket, or other suitable container and mix well. The signer draws a card without showing it to the other players, and silently signs whatever is on it.

- Other players try to find the corresponding picture on their card and mark it with a piece of cereal or a crayon. (*Hint:* If you cover the cards with clear contact paper and mark them with washable crayons, you can use them again!)

- The first player to complete a row shouts "SIGNO!"

I Spy with My Little Eye . . .

Do you remember playing "I Spy" on long car trips when you were a kid? This is my new version, adapted for signing. You can do this in the house, the yard, the park, and yes, even on lengthy road trips.

What to Do

- Each person takes a turn being the signer, while the rest guess what's being signed.

- The signer looks around, and when she's found something to sign, she says, "I spy with my little eye something that has the sign _____," and signs it to the other players. If you want to include more signing, you can also sign **SEE** (for "spy") and **EYE** (point to eye).

- Everyone attempts to guess what the sign is.

- You can either have the person who guesses correctly be the next signer, or just continue around the group, giving each player a turn.

SEE. The first two finger form a "V" shape and point to the eyes, then move forward to represent seeing.

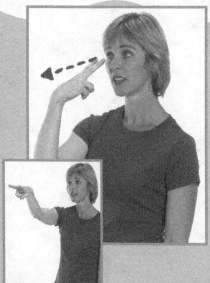

LOOK. The first two fingers form a "V" and point at the eyes, then move away toward what you're looking at.

147

Chapter 9

Creative Signing with Daily Routines

igning with daily routines is very important, because both you and your baby benefit a lot from using the same signs repeatedly throughout the day. For your child, seeing the same gestures over and over helps him learn to recognize the movements and produce the signs himself. For you, repeating gestures in certain recurring situations helps you make signing throughout the day a consistent habit. Eventually, it will feel so natural that you may find yourself mistakenly signing to those who don't understand it—for example, I often catch myself signing **THANK YOU** to the checkout person at my local supermarket!

Often, however, I hear parents in my classes complain that their baby "just won't pay attention" to certain signs that they're using, and this seems to be especially true of signing with daily routines. The parents, of course, are very motivated to get their baby to learn to express basic needs, but the child, on the other hand, finds these routine signs a little boring. After all, crying usually gets Baby what she wants, so why should she try something new?

What parents need is a way to put another spin on this—a way to get out of the rut and make routine signs more fun and motivating to the baby. In this chapter, we're going to explore some creative ways to bring the fun back, so get ready to change that diaper and have some laughs in the process!

My niece Ruby signs WASH to her baby sister, Rachel

Taking Care of Teddy

Maybe you've been signing **EAT** and **DIAPER CHANGE** for months now, but your baby just won't do the signs. He certainly seems to *recognize* them, but for some reason he won't make them himself. This is one of the chief frustrations I hear from parents, who often begin to lose heart at this point and feel that maybe *their* baby is one who "just won't sign." This isn't the case, however, since all children will sign. It's just a matter of motivating them properly by giving them signs to express what they really want to say!

The next time you feed your baby, have one of his favorite dolls or stuffed animals seated close by on a chair or the table. Sometime during the meal, tell him that Dolly or Teddy is hungry, too. Say and sign, "Teddy (or Dolly) wants to **EAT**. Let's give him some **FOOD**," and then pretend to feed the toy. Chances are, your baby will suddenly become very interested in signing **EAT** when it's all about his doll!

Sometime when you're near the changing table, maybe before or after getting your baby into a new diaper, tell him, "Dolly (or Teddy) needs a **DIAPER CHANGE**." Change Dolly or Teddy on the floor and let your child help. We do this in my classes, and you'd be amazed by how

Continued . . .

babies who are usually fussy about the process suddenly become fascinated with helping the doll. Something that they previously regarded as literally a "pain in the heinie" is suddenly a fun game!

Try doing this with other routines such as getting dressed, climbing into the car seat, having a bath (use a plastic doll in tub or basin), brushing teeth, and any others that you can think of.

 CHANGE and EAT

DOLL. The bent forefinger is pulled twice down the nose.

BEAR. The hands are crossed over the chest and make scratching motions.

Sign Me a Story

Signing along with books makes reading more fun and interactive for your baby and provides an opportunity to sign about things that are out of the realm of day-to-day experiences. Combining pictures with spoken vocabulary and signs reinforces new ideas for your child and gives her a way to actively participate by commenting on the story and pictures.

Once in a while, when you read a story together, try seating your baby across from you, in her bouncy seat, stroller, car seat, or swing. This allows her to see your facial expressions and signs, frees up your hands, and enables you to see her reaction as you tell the story—which is a lot more fun than looking at the back of her head (even though the backs of babies' heads are very cute!).

When you read aloud, remember that you don't have to go through the entire book or even tell the same story as the author. Babies have short attention spans, so pointing at the pictures (or letting your child point to them) and talking about what you see generally works better than trying to follow the text word for word. Most kids will try turn the pages before you're ready or pull the book out of your hands anyway, so you'll seldom

Continued . . .

have time to do more than make a comment or two about each picture.

You can use signs with most picture books, but there are a few types that lend themselves especially well to this process:

- Books with one concept per page, which makes it very clear what you're signing about. *Brown Bear, Brown Bear, What Do You See?* by Bill Martin, Jr., illustrated by Eric Carle, is a great example.

- Books that repeat the same concept on each page, which gives you the opportunity to reinforce one sign through repetition. *Goodnight Moon* and *The Runaway Bunny* by Margaret Wise Brown, illustrated by Clement Hurd, are good choices. Both have bunnies on most pages, and *Goodnight Moon* has a mouse hiding on each page as well.

- Vocabulary-building books with pictures of many objects on each page are great for signed- and verbal-vocabulary building. You can also play a "let's-find" game by signing an object and asking your child to find it on the page. There are many of these books available, such as *Baby's Book of*

Animals by Roger Priddy or *Richard Scarry's Best Word Book Ever.*

- American Sign Language books especially for children are also available. You can find them at the library and at local and online bookstores. These are wonderful because they often show pictures of kids signing, are based on subjects of special interest to children, and include signs along with the pictures on each page. For a list of children's signing books, see the "Resources" section.

You don't need to limit yourself only to reading children's books with your baby, however—anything with engaging pictures will do:

- Find pictures of babies and children in parenting magazines.

- Look at photos of food in gourmet magazines.

- Try a copy of *National Geographic* for wildlife photos (screen the content first for scary pictures!).

Continued . . .

• Magazines for cat, dog, horse, boat, and car lovers are great for showing many versions of the same thing. Leafing through a copy of *Dog Fancy* is a fun way to show just how many different kind of **DOGS** there are—from Chihuahuas to Great Danes!

BOOK. Hold hands flat, with palms together. Open hands like the covers of a book.

READ. The first two fingers form a "V," representing the eyes, which scan the flat palm of the opposite hand, as if "reading" it.

Bath-Time Fun

Most babies love their bath, and as
a daily routine, it provides an excellent
opportunity to use the same signs each day in a fun way.
This is a perfect example of how it takes no extra time
on your part to play and sign with your baby. You have to
be right there while he's in the tub anyway, so you may
as well have fun and learn.

When it's time to get clean, turn on the water and
say and sign, "It's time to have a **BATH!**" or "It's time
to get **IN** the **BATH!**" Then immediately lift him into the
tub. While he's splashing around, you can play and sign in
many ways.

What to Do

- Say and sign "**WARM**" and "**COLD**" as you
  alternate turning on the corresponding taps,
  or fill plastic containers with **WARM** and **COLD**
  water and let your baby splash in them.

- Sign about various bath toys you may have,
  such as a **DUCK, BOAT, FISH,** or **DOLL.**

Continued . . .

- Splash the water as you say and sign "**SPLASH.**"

- Show him that a washcloth or soft toy is **DRY**— and then make it **WET!**

- Run a bubble bath and say and sign "**BUBBLES**" as you play with them!

- Say and sign, "**ALL DONE**" or "Time to get **OUT**" when you're finished.

- Ask "**WHERE** is your **(NOSE, EAR, ARM, BELLY BUTTON)?**" and then point to the corresponding body part with your index finger and say, "There it is!"

- Play "**WASH** the **BABY,**" or sign body parts with a doll as described above.

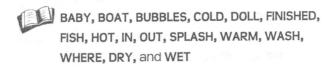 BABY, BOAT, BUBBLES, COLD, DOLL, FINISHED, FISH, HOT, IN, OUT, SPLASH, WARM, WASH, WHERE, DRY, and WET

BATH. The fists scrub up and down the torso, parallel to each other.

DUCK. The hand is held near the mouth, facing out, while the first two fingers open and close on top of the thumb, imitating a duck's bill.

159

Diapering and Signing

Besides providing an opportunity to use the same signs repeatedly throughout the day, signing about changing diapers can offer playful diversions and help make your baby more cooperative. **CHANGE, DIAPER, WET,** and **POOP** are good signs to use.

Often, babies put up a big protest at changing time, which can make the process very difficult! As parents, we can't imagine what all the fuss is about—why on earth does she seem to *want* to stay in a wet or dirty diaper? To understand this, you need to look at it from her perspective: Imagine yourself busily doing something important to you (such as typing an e-mail), when your spouse comes into the room and—without a word—grabs you by the arm and starts pulling you out the front door. That sounds annoying, right?

Now, imagine your baby happily playing on the floor when you come up behind her and whisk her away to the changing table, with no explanation. See the similarity?

When you get a whiff from your baby's diaper and realize that she needs to be changed, try giving her some warning by squatting down in front of her and saying, "It's time for a **DIAPER CHANGE!**" You'll probably be surprised by how much more cooperative she can be when you give her the chance.

Here are more ideas for signing at changing time:

What to Do

- Sing and sign a song after the new diaper is on, but while your baby is still on the changing table. Stop and start the song at intervals, asking if she wants **MORE** singing. She'll come to anticipate and look forward to this game!

- Tape pictures of things that you're learning signs for near the changing table—such as family members, animals, and familiar objects—and use these signs as you point to and talk about the pictures. Your baby will be entertained and less likely to squirm.

- Have some small toys in a basket near the changing area. Hand them to your child one at a time as you change her diaper, using the sign as you say the name of the toy—such as **CAR, DOLL,** or **BEAR**—to give her something to focus on and reduce squirming.

Continued . . .

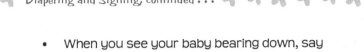
- When you see your baby bearing down, say "Good girl! You're making a **POOP** in your diaper!" Becoming conscious of this process is an important first step to future potty training.

 BEAR, CAR, DIAPER, DOLL, MORE, and **WET**

CHANGE. The two fists are held together, facing opposite directions, with knuckles touching. Both hands pivot in opposite directions in order to change places.

POOP. Pull the thumb out of the bottom of the opposite closed fist.

Signing and Dressing

Putting clothes on and taking them off are routines that many parents overlook as far as signing goes, but both occasions offer a great opportunity to use certain signs on a daily basis. You can use the signs for specific items of clothing, as well as those such as **CLOTHES, ON, OFF, CLEAN, HOT, WARM, COLD,** and **DIRTY.** The next time you dress your baby, try some of these ideas:

What to Do

- Try holding up each item of clothing before you put it on, and enthusiastically say and sign its name. You can say, "This is baby's **SHIRT!**" or you can add adjectives to describe the item, if you like; for example: "This is baby's **BLUE SHIRT!**"

- If my son is squirming while I'm trying to dress him, I often find that picking up his socks (for instance) and *very* enthusiastically saying and signing "**SOCKS**" gets his attention and fools him

Continued . . .

into thinking that having them on his feet is a real treat. This magic only works for a moment, but it's usually long enough to do the trick!

- If you have to change a soiled shirt, say and sign to your baby that his **SHIRT** is **DIRTY.** Then show him a clean one, and say and sign "**CLEAN.**"

- Whenever it's time to take off or put on clothing, sign **ON** and **OFF;** for example: "Time to take **OFF CLOTHES**" or "Now your clothes are **OFF.** Time to put **ON** pajamas!"

- Look out the window and talk and sign about what kind of day it will be and what clothes will be appropriate; for instance: "It's **COLD** outside—we need to put on a **WARM SHIRT.**"

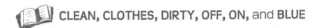 CLEAN, CLOTHES, DIRTY, OFF, ON, and BLUE

SHIRT. Indicate the shirt by pulling on the front of it. You can use one or both hands.

SOCKS. The index fingers point downward and alternately run against each other, like knitting needles making socks.

165

Creative Signing for Mealtimes

Meals are a great time for family members to bond as they discuss their days, yet for a baby who doesn't talk yet, this can be a time of frustration. Everyone else is engaged in conversation and she'd like nothing more than to join in, but alas, her contributions are pretty much limited to shouting, banging her cup and utensils, and throwing food on the floor.

When a baby can sign, however, the dynamic is entirely different. She no longer needs to "misbehave" to participate at the dinner table—she now has a positive means of getting attention, and the thrilled response she gets from the rest of the family is great for her self-esteem. As Baby happily joins in the dinnertime conversation, the signing works its magic and dinnertime is far more relaxing.

When you're feeding your baby, of course it's a good idea to use basic mealtime gestures, such as **EAT, DRINK, MORE,** and **FINISHED.** Signing along with routines *consistently* is essential for your child's comprehension. But it's also important not to bore her to death by just doing the "same old, same old" every day, so try these ideas to make mealtime signing more interesting:

What to Do

- Use different-colored spoons and bowls, and sign about the colors.

- Put flowers on the table and sign **FLOWERS.**

- Have all family members sign **PLEASE, THANK YOU,** and **YOU'RE WELCOME.**

- Sign and talk about other family members eating: "Daddy is **EATING!**"

- Use place mats and other dinnerware featuring things that you can sign about, such as animals.

- Sign about things that you can see outside the window or around the room.

- Have everyone "toast" often, saying "Cheers!" and then sign **DRINK** when you all take a sip.

- Sign about the food being **YUMMY, HOT,** or **COLD.**

- Sign a song together. (We used to do "Old MacDonald" at every meal!)

Continued ...

 COLD, DRINK, EAT, FINISHED, FLOWERS, HOT, and **MORE**

PLEASE. The open palm touches the chest and moves in a circular motion.

THANK YOU and **YOU'RE WELCOME.** The fingertips of the flat hand touch the lips and then move out and down toward the person being thanked, representing nice words coming from the mouth.

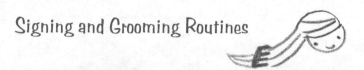

Signing and Grooming Routines

Daily grooming routines and the various paraphernalia involved are very intriguing to babies. Even those with no hair or teeth are fascinated by hair- and toothbrushes, lotion and shampoo bottles, and the like.

What to Do

- Sign **BRUSH TEETH** when you're brushing your baby's teeth or your own.

- Sign **WASH** when it's time to wash his hands or sing and sign a hand-washing song!

- Sign **BRUSH** or **COMB** when brushing hair—either his or yours.

- Give him a clean, empty shampoo bottle to play with (discard any small lids or parts that could pose a choking hazard) and sign **SHAMPOO.**

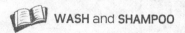 WASH and SHAMPOO

Continued . . .

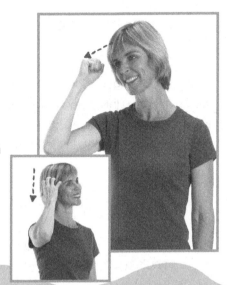

BRUSH or COMB HAIR. For **BRUSH,** mimic the act of holding the handle of a brush and then using it. For **COMB,** comb hair with fingers.

BRUSH TEETH. Mimic brushing teeth with index finger.

Bedtime Signing

Bedtime is a great opportunity to use
signs with your baby. For many families,
it's often one of the few chances for
them let go of the cares and worries of the day and
spend some special time relaxing and cuddling together.

What to Do

- Sing and sign a lullaby.

- Sign along with a bedtime story.

- Talk and sign about stuffed toys as you play
  with them.

- Point out things in your baby's bedroom and
  sign about them.

- Sign **BLANKET** and **PACIFIER** as you give these
  to her.

- Sign **KISS** and **HUG.**

- Say and sign a little **PRAYER.**

- Say and sign "Time to go to **BED**" and "Go to
  SLEEP."

Continued . . .

HUG, KISS, PACIFIER, and PRAY

BED. (Use this for **SLEEP**, too.) Rest your head on your hand, as if it's a pillow.

BLANKET. The downturned hands grasp and pull up an imaginary blanket.

172

Staying Safe: Setting and Communicating Limits with Signs

Signing is great for getting baby what he wants, but it can also be used to help keep him safe. Simply moving him away from danger works when you're close at hand, but taking the time to teach him to respond to your requests is safer and actually makes life easier for you in the long run, since a big part of your daily routine involves shielding your child from danger.

Wouldn't it be nice if you could sign and say "**NO**," and your baby would simply crawl away from the dishwasher you're in the middle of unloading? Of course I'm not suggesting signing as a substitute for close parental supervision and thorough baby proofing, but it's a great tool to add to your other precautions. Read on to find out how signing can be used to teach your baby about safety.

What to Do

- When your baby is crawling toward something dangerous, or is about to pick it up, sign and firmly say "**NO**" or "**STOP**" and move him away. If he immediately tries to come back (to that

Continued . . .

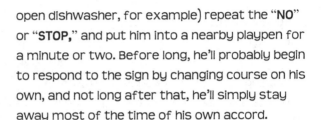

open dishwasher, for example) repeat the "**NO**" or "**STOP**," and put him into a nearby playpen for a minute or two. Before long, he'll probably begin to respond to the sign by changing course on his own, and not long after that, he'll simply stay away most of the time of his own accord.

- When you encounter dangerous things—such open trenches, broken glass or playground equipment, cacti, biting bugs, and the like—point them out to your baby and say and sign "**OUCH!**" **(PAIN)**, "**NO TOUCH!**" You may even want to pretend to touch a cactus, for example, and say and sign "**OUCH**" and "**CRY**."

- When someone is cooking on the stove, you're using the fireplace at home, or you're near a campfire or barbecue, show your baby these dangers from a safe distance and sign **HOT, NO TOUCH,** and **OUCH! (PAIN).** Be fairly dramatic with these signs. Using an alarmed facial expression when saying "**HOT**" or "**NO TOUCH,**" or a pained look when saying "**OUCH!**" **(PAIN),** is important to the meaning.

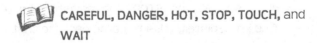 CAREFUL, DANGER, HOT, STOP, TOUCH, and WAIT

NO. The first two fingers close down on the thumb. This is a variation of the finger spelling of no.

PAIN. The two index fingers tap together several times at the location of the pain, representing throbbing nerve endings. The face should have a pained expression.

chapter 10

Signing Crafts

You may wonder what signing crafts are, and in fact, the topic never occurred to me until people started sending me ideas for this book. I was delighted to receive a couple of very original and creative projects, but realized that they needed a chapter all their own.

If you have older toddlers, they may be able to participate in some of these. Otherwise, make the crafts yourself to enjoy with your baby, and to create memories of her signing for the entire family to enjoy for years to come.

"My First Signs" Book

This is a fun and easy craft that a parent can do alone or with the "help" of a toddler.

What You'll Need

- Photos of family members, friends, and/or pets

- A camera (digital is easiest)

- Pictures of objects that you're teaching signs for (these can be cut out of magazines)

- Pictures of yourself signing or copies of signs from this book, if desired

- A glue stick

- Washable colored pens or crayons

- Construction paper or card stock

- Page protectors or large Ziploc bags

- A three-ring binder or three pieces of yarn.

What to Do

• Paste pictures from magazines or photos
  of people on each page. You can also include
  a photo of you or your child making the
  appropriate sign next to it.

• Write the word that goes with the sign and
  picture(s) with colored pens or crayons.

• Slip the completed pages into plastic protectors
  or large Ziploc bags (punch holes in the edges if
  you choose this option).

• Put the pages into a three-ring binder or create
  a soft book by tying loops of yarn through the
  holes to hold the sheets together.

Mini "My First Signs" Books

These are so simple that you'll probably want to make several with different themes, such as family, bedtime, or favorite signs. If your baby goes to day care, send these books along with him. The familiar images from home are a fun way for caregivers to interact with and comfort your child. (You might want to put copied illustrations or photos of the corresponding signs on the facing pages in order to help the staff learn them.)

Idea contributed by: Brandy Brass-Rafeek, owner of "Sweet Signs" www.sweetsigns.ca

What You'll Need

- Mini photo albums with plastic sleeves
- Clear tape
- A camera (digital is easiest)

What to Do

- Take photos of familiar objects, people, or situations that you want to sign. For example, for a bedtime book, you could take a picture of your baby's crib, someone reading him a story, and him taking a bath or having his teeth brushed. Alternatively, you could just photograph the crib, the tub, a book, and a toothbrush.

- If you like, you can take photos of yourself signing these words or make copies from this book.

- Print or develop the pictures.

- Sort the photos into the order you want and slide them into the plastic sleeves. If you're including illustrations or photos of the signs, put them on the page facing each sign so that the reader sees the object and the gesture at the same time.

- Tape the edges of the sleeves shut so that your baby can't get the pictures out.

- Look at these albums with your child and talk and sign about the photos!

Signing Memory Book

I came up with this idea when I realized how little space there was in my children's baby books to record their language development. In my eyes, their signing milestones were far more thrilling than most of the other events that were given space ("When baby first ate dirt," for instance!). I only found at most a couple of pages devoted to first words in most baby books—with many having only a couple of lines available—and of course I wanted to record first words *and* signs.

You can make this project as simple or complex as you like. Some parents will prefer to use a plain notebook to jot down what their baby has learned, funny signing stories, and maybe glue in a few photos. Ambitious moms who've caught the "scrapbook bug" may choose to make an elaborate version using an expandable album, including photos mounted on decorated pages in plastic protectors.

Either way, this signing scrapbook can become a memento that you'll look through for years to come.

What You'll Need

Most of these can be found anywhere that craft supplies are sold.

- A large notebook, blank journal, three-ring binder, or scrapbook album

- Sheets of acid-free card stock and plastic page protectors (unless you're using a notebook or journal)

- Photo-mounting adhesive, such as tape or glue

- Miscellaneous scrapbook paraphernalia, such as stickers, adhesive letters, die-cut shapes, and so on

- Personal memorabilia, such as photos of your baby signing, pictures of things that she can sign the names of, and personal stories of her signing. Capturing her making the gestures herself is best done with a digital camera that can take a series of pictures in quick succession (you can erase the ones you don't want). Try interacting normally with her while someone

Continued . . .

else takes photos. Older kids will often produce signs when prompted, which makes this a lot easier!

Assembling the Memory-Book Pages

- Mount a photo on a page and write a short story about your baby using this sign. For example, glue in a shot of her signing **BIRD** or a picture of a **BIRD** from a magazine, and then write a short story about her using the sign.

- Once you've put in your main subject picture(s) and story, decorate your page with colored pens, stickers, pressed flowers, or anything else that you like. Then, if you're using an album, insert the sheet into a plastic page protector and put it into the binder.

- You can make as many pages as you like—one for every sweet memory of your child using her signs!

"I Love You" Hand or Foot Photo

This sweet craft makes a beautiful keepsake that will be cherished forever. It will look lovely on your baby's wall or dresser, and it also makes a very special and original gift for family members.

This idea was contributed by signing teacher Tracey Sweetapple of Vernon, British Columbia. Tracey has a master's degree in special education, is fluent in American Sign Language, and signs with her baby girl. (Find out more about Tracey and her classes at **www.sweetapplesigns.com**.)

What You'll Need

- A digital or regular camera and black-and-white film

- Picture frames with matting (pewter or black look great)

Continued . . .

What to Do

- Take a close-up picture of your own hand signing **I LOVE YOU,** with your baby grasping your thumb or pinkie finger. Alternatively, you can balance your baby's foot on your signing hand. If you're using a digital camera, use the black-and-white or sepia setting. If your camera doesn't have these options, you can change your printer options to produce the image in "gray scale."

- Print out your pictures or get them developed at a lab that processes black-and-white film.

- Mount your photos in the frames.

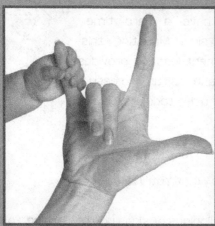

© Bill Pitcher, Golden BC Photography

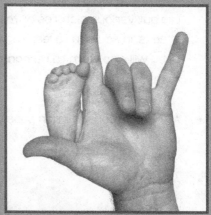

© Bill Pitcher, Golden BC Photography

Sign of the Week Collage

Many parents have a hard time remembering to sign. Mounting this project in a prominent location provides a great reminder, and it's fun and easy to make. If you have older toddlers, you can let them help!

What You'll Need

- Magazine clippings of signs you're learning. For example, if you're working on the sign for **DOG,** clip out various pictures of many different breeds. In addition to learning the gesture, your baby will also learn to recognize that there are many kinds of dogs!

- A sheet of construction paper or cardstock or a paper plate

- A glue stick

What to Do

- Glue clippings representing the "sign of the week" onto the paper or plate.

- Hang the collage on the wall near the changing table, high chair, or another place that you and your child will see it often.

- Several times a day, point to the pictures and sign about them.

Mealtime Signs Place Mat

Do you have trouble remembering to sign at meals? This fun little craft will help keep the high-chair tray or table neater while it reminds you to keep your hands moving.

What You'll Need

- Magazine clippings with pictures of foods, drinks, and people eating

- Pictures of mealtime signs, either photos of yourself signing or pictures copied from this book—or you can draw them yourself

- A sheet of construction paper or card stock, cut into a rectangle

- A glue stick

- A felt-tip marker

- Clear contact paper for "laminating"

What to Do

- Glue the magazine images and their corresponding sign illustrations onto paper.

- Write the name of each sign next to the picture with a marker or crayon.

- Cover your place mat with clear contact paper.

My son, Aiden, signs FINISHED.

Flash Cards

You can purchase ASL flash cards for signing with babies, but you might also enjoy making a few of your own. The advantage of a homemade set is that you can personalize it by using pictures of familiar things and family members. For example, you could use a picture of your baby's grandmother for the **GRANDMA** flash card or a photo of your family pet for the **CAT** or **DOG** card.

A note on flash card use: Younger children learn signing most effectively when it's included during normal and relaxed interactions, so there's a right way and a wrong way to use this tool with babies. Choose a few cards and look at them with your little one as if they're a picture book, talking and signing about the objects on them. Don't make him finish all the cards—stop when he seems to be losing interest. It's best not to quiz him or pressure him to perform, because if you make this seem like work, he'll be less motivated to do it with you.

What You'll Need

- Magazine clippings

- Photos of family members, pets, toys, and household items

- Pictures of signs, either photos of yourself making the gestures, copies of illustrations from this book, or your own drawings

- Blank index cards or card stock, cut into the appropriate size

- A glue stick

- Felt-tip pens or crayons

- Clear contact paper for "laminating"

What to Do

- Glue photos or magazine clippings onto cards.

- On the opposite side, glue the picture of corresponding sign.

- Write the appropriate word on the side with the sign.

- "Laminate" your cards with clear contact paper.

193

Greeting Cards

What better way to say "Thank you," "Happy birthday," or "Happy holidays" than a homemade card from you and your child? These original and heartfelt greetings are sure to be appreciated by everyone who's lucky enough to receive them.

What You'll Need

- Colored card stock

- Photos of you and/or your child signing—use the **THANK YOU** sign for thank-you notes and the **HAPPY** sign for holiday and birthday cards. You can look up more signs on the ASL Browser at **www.commtechlab.msu.edu/sites/aslweb/browser.htm.**

- Colored markers

- A glue stick

- Decorative bits and pieces, such as scraps of colored paper, small pieces of ribbon, pressed flowers, and the like

What to Do

- Cut and fold card stock to make a card.
- Glue in a photo of your child signing.
- Write your message on the card.
- Finish by embellishing it with decorative bits and pieces.

HAPPY. The flat hand pats the chest repeatedly with an upward stroking movement, representing happy feelings bubbling up.

THANK YOU/ YOU'RE WELCOME. The fingertips of the flat hand touch the lips and then move out and down toward the person being thanked, representing nice words coming from the mouth.

✷ ✷ ✷ ✷ ✷ ✷ ✷ ✷ ✷ ✷ ✷ ✷ ✷ ✷ ✷ ✷ ✷

SIGNO Cards
(For Signing BINGO; see p. 144 for
play instructions)

There are a couple of ways to
make your SIGNO cards. You can use a
computer to create them and insert graphics, or you
can make them by hand with stickers and pens. Choose
whichever is easiest for you.

Computer-Savvy Method

What you'll need:

- A computer program that will draw graphs
  and insert clip art (such as Microsoft Word or
  Publisher)

- A printer, preferably a color one

- Printer paper

- Clear contact paper

- Crayons or pieces of breakfast cereal to mark
  off winning squares

What to do:

- Using your computer program, create a table with five rows and five columns.

- Type "FREE" in the center box, if you want a free space.

- In the other boxes, insert illustrations for signs that your baby knows by clicking "insert," then "picture," and then "clip art." Type the word that you want into the search box and select an appropriate image.

- Type the name of each sign below its illustration.

- Make two copies of the card and "laminate" with contact paper.

- Make "draw cards" by cutting up one big card into individual signs.

Continued . . .

Low-Tech Method

What you'll need:

- White card stock

- Kids' stickers with pictures of things that your baby knows signs for

- Markers

- Clear contact paper

- Crayons or pieces of breakfast cereal to mark off winning squares

What to do:

- Use a marker to draw two square tables with five rows and five columns each onto pieces of card stock, making them big enough that you can fit stickers and descriptive words in each square. I recommend making the table *at least* 8" square.

- Write "FREE" in the center square if you want a free space.

- Put stickers in remaining the squares, or glue in magazine clippings or drawings, and use a marker to write the word that goes with each picture below it.

- "Laminate" both cards with contact paper.

- Make "draw cards" by cutting up one table into individual signs.

Note: If you plan on playing with more than two people—that is, more than just you and your child—you'll need to make different cards with the signs in a different order. If you play with grown-ups, you might want to have more signs than there are spaces, so that it's harder to win. (In this case, some cards won't have every sign.)

Chapter 11

Sing and Sign

Signing along with songs is not only fun, it can also be very helpful during transitions from one activity to another, which are often difficult for young children. Signing an appropriate song alerts your baby that a change is taking place, while encouraging them to participate in it. Ask any preschool teacher—they use songs in this way every day!

Hand Washing

Try singing the following songs just before taking your child to the sink to wash her hands at mealtimes or after playing in the dirt or doing messy craft activities. You can continue to sing (without signing) as you actually help wash her hands.

Hand Washing Song #1
*(Sing to the tune of "Row, Row, Row Your Boat," signing **WASH HANDS** throughout.)*

WASH, WASH, WASH your **HANDS!**
Play our handy game—
Rub and scrub, scrub and rub,
Germs go down the drain, hey!

WASH, WASH, WASH your **HANDS!**
Play our handy game—
Rub and scrub, scrub and rub,
DIRT goes down the drain, hey!

Hand Washing Song #2

*(Sing to the tune of "Row, Row, Row Your Boat," signing **WASH HANDS** throughout.)*

WASH, WASH, WASH your **HANDS**
Till they're nice and **CLEAN.**
Scrubby, scrubby, scrubby, scrubby!
Now they're nice and **CLEAN.**

WASH HANDS. Rub hands all over each other, as if washing them.

Clean-Up Time

Getting your baby to help put toys away can be very challenging. Using a "clean-up" song encourages him to participate, by making it feel like a game.

You can also use signs as you encourage him to put things **IN** the toy box or cupboard or **ON** the shelf, praising him lavishly as he does.

My Toys Are All Over the Bedroom
(Sung to the chorus of "My Bonnie Lies Over the Ocean.")

My **TOYS** are all over the bedroom.
I **PLAY** with my **TOYS** all day.
My **TOYS** are all over the bedroom.
Let's **CLEAN UP** and put **TOYS** away.

CLEAN UP, CLEAN UP!
HELP Mommy put all the toys away.
CLEAN UP, CLEAN UP!
HELP Mommy **CLEAN UP** today.

Everybody Clean Up

(Chant in a singsong voice, making up your own tune.
*For **EVERYBODY,** use the natural gesture of swinging your*
pointer finger in an arc around the room, indicating
everyone present.)

CLEAN UP, CLEAN UP,
EVERYONE across the land!
CLEAN UP, CLEAN UP,
EVERYBODY lend a hand (sign HELP)!

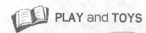

PLAY and **TOYS**

WASH (CLEAN UP). The
fist of the action hand
scrubs the opposite
open palm in a circular
motion, as if scrubbing
something clean.

Continued . . .

HELP. ASL version: The action hand is formed into a fist and placed on top of the flat base hand. Both rise up together, as if the flat hand is helping lift the fist. The thumb of the action hand may point upward, and can be used to indicate who needs help by pointing as it rises.

HELP. Non-ASL version: Non-ASL version: This is recommended for very young children by Joseph Garcia in *Sign with Your Baby.* Both flat hands pat the chest, which is easier for parents to recognize when done by younger babies.

206

Changing-Time Songs

The transition from a dirty to clean diaper can be an especially difficult one for babies. Most of them just don't seem to feel that the benefits outweigh the inconvenience (and indignity, perhaps?) of being changed.

Sometimes your baby just appreciates a little advance notice before being whisked off to the changing table. Can you imagine if someone just came over and started pulling your pants off without any warning? This could be pretty annoying, especially in mixed company!

Try the following songs to alert your baby to changing time.

Baby Needs a Diaper Change
*(Sing to the tune of "Mary Had a Little Lamb"
or "Do You Know the Muffin Man?")*

Baby needs a diaper **CHANGE,**
(A) diaper **CHANGE,**
(A) diaper **CHANGE!**
Baby needs a diaper **CHANGE!**
Let's go have a **CHANGE!**

Continued . . .

Change It! Change It!
(Sing to the tune of "Camptown Races.")

Baby's diaper is all **WET** (has a **POOP**)—
CHANGE it! **CHANGE** it!
Baby's diaper is all **WET** (has a **POOP**)—
Time to **CHANGE** it now!

Take the **WET (POOPY)** one off,
Put the **DRY (CLEAN)** one on!

Baby's diaper is all **WET** (has a **POOP**),
Let's go **CHANGE** it now!

 CLEAN, DRY, and WET

CHANGE. The two fists are held together, facing opposite directions, with knuckles touching. Both hand pivot in opposite directions in order to change places.

POOP. Pull the thumb out of the bottom of the opposite closed fist.

Bath Time

All I have to do is turn on the water and my babies come tearing down the hall and try to crawl into the tub. I know that there are other children, however, who have to be chased into the bathroom. Either way, a bath-time song is a fun way to get them in the mood.

Baby's Bath-Time Song
(Sing to the tune of "Camptown Races."
Indicate body parts by pointing to them.)

WATER, WATER in the tub,
BATH TIME, BATH TIME!
WATER, WATER in the tub,
Baby's **BATH TIME**'s here!

WASH the baby's **NOSE.**
WASH the baby's **TOES.**

WATER, WATER in the tub,
Baby's **BATH TIME**'s here!

(Sing again, substituting other body parts)

WATER. The first three fingers form a "W" and tap the chin twice.

BATH TIME (BATH). The fists scrub up and down the torso, parallel to each other.

Continued . . .

Dirty Laundry
(Sing to the tune of "Mary Had a Little Lamb.")

Baby's **SHIRT** is **DIRTY** now,
DIRTY now, **DIRTY** now.
Baby's **SHIRT** is **DIRTY** now.
Let **MOMMY** take it **OFF!**

Baby's **PANTS** are **DIRTY,** too,
DIRTY too, **DIRTY** too.
Baby's **PANTS** are **DIRTY,** too.
Let **MOMMY** take them **OFF!**

Baby's **DIAPER** is all **WET,**
is all **WET,** is all **WET.**
Baby's **DIAPER** is all **WET.**
Let **MOMMY** take it **OFF!**

Baby's ready for a **BATH,**
For a **BATH,** for a **BATH.**
Baby's ready for a **BATH**
To get all nice and **CLEAN!**

 BATH, CLEAN, MOMMY, OFF, PANTS, and WET

DIRTY. Hold hand under chin and wiggle fingers. (You're in dirt up to your neck!)

SHIRT. Indicate the shirt by pulling on the front of it. You can use one or both hands.

213

Clothes and Dressing

Getting your baby dressed can be a struggle sometimes. Try singing a song about putting on clothes to engage him.

The Getting Dressed Song

*(Sing to the tune of "Frère Jacques," substituting your child's name for "baby" if you like. You can also add descriptive terms for the item of clothing [**BLUE** shirt, **TRUCK** shirt].)*

Here is baby's **SHIRT.**
Here is baby's **SHIRT.**
Put it **ON**, put it **ON!**
Baby needs a **SHIRT.**
Baby needs a **SHIRT.**
Put it **ON**, put it **ON!**

Here are baby's **PANTS.**
Here are baby's **PANTS.**
Put them **ON**, put them **ON!**
Baby needs some **PANTS.**
Baby needs some **PANTS.**
Put them **ON,** put them **ON!**

Repeat with other items of clothing.

 DIAPER, SHOES, and SOCKS

PANTS. Go through the motion of pulling up pants.

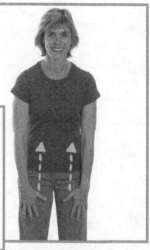

SHIRT. Indicate the front of the shirt by pulling on it. You can use one or both hands.

part III

the signs

The Manual Alphabet

Don't freak out on me now—I don't expect you to start finger spelling to your baby! She's too little to learn to spell yet, and although she'll be able to form some of the letters before she can talk, she probably won't have the coordination to do others correctly until at least the age of three.

I've included this manual alphabet for a couple of reasons, the most important being that I sometimes use terminology relating to it when describing signs. For example, I may tell you that the sign for PLAY is made by shaking the "Y" hands, or that the sign for TOILET is made by shaking the "T" hand. I always strive to describe the hand shapes in the simplest possible terms, and sometimes, using the manual-alphabet letter is the clearest way. As you look at the photos of the signs and read the descriptions, you'll naturally begin to learn how some of the letters are formed.

Another reason that I've included this section is that many parents have asked me if there's a way to make up a sign for their child's name or the names of other family members, friends, or pets.

In the deaf community, name signs are traditionally given by a deaf person and often incorporate the first letter of the person's name and some physical or personality attribute of whoever's being named.

The deaf create name signs as a way of identifying other people within their commumnity, and most people within the deaf community are adamant that these kinds of signs only be given by a deaf individual.

If you aren't lucky enough to have a deaf friend or family member around to bestow this honor upon you, there is an accepted way to make up a "name indicator." Simply sign the first letter of the person's name over your heart. If it's Grandma Barbara, for example, you can sign GRANDMA and then the sign for "B" over your heart.

Keep in mind that this is not a "name sign." You are simple refering to the person by their initial, which is something we do in spoken language as well, for example, calling someone J.D. or Aunt B.

One of the gestures that my son uses most is his sister's name indicator. He makes it when he kisses her, hears her voice, shows me something that belongs to her, or wants to know where she is. I'm sure your family will find these alphabet signs just as useful.

The Manual Alphabet

Signing Vocabulary

AGAIN

The fingertips of the curved action hand come down in an arc to touch the upturned palm of the base hand.

AIRPLANE

The "Y" hand, with the index finger extended and palm down, moves up and away from the body, representing the wings and fuselage of an airplane flying through the sky.

ALLIGATOR

The fingers of both hands bend at the knuckles, forming "claw hands." The hands open and close on each other, like an alligator's jaws snapping open and shut.

ANIMAL

The fingertips of both hands rest on the chest as the hands move back and forth toward each other. This represents animals' breathing.

APPLE

The knuckle of the bent
index finger twists on the
cheek near the corner of
the mouth, representing
the stem being twisted
out of an apple.

BABY

One arm cradles the
other and moves from
side to side, as if
rocking a baby.

 BABYSITTER/ NANNY

Use the sign for **KEEP:** Rest one "K" hand on top of the other at an angle. ("K" is signed by holding up the first two fingers with the middle finger slanted in at an angle.) Now, move both hands in a small circle in front of you. This changes the meaning to **CARE.**

BALL

The curved hands, with fingers spread, bounce toward each other, as if holding a ball.

BANANA

Go through the motions of peeling a banana. The extended index finger of the base hand represents the banana, while the fingertips of the action hand pull down the skin.

BATH

The fists scrub up and down the torso, parallel to each other.

BEAR

The two "claw hands" are crossed over the chest and make scratching motions, like a bear scratching itself.

BEAUTIFUL

The open hand starts on one side of the face and swoops up and around, closing as it reaches the chin.

BED
(use for SLEEP, too).

Rest your head on your hand, as if it's a pillow. You can use one or both hands.

BELL

The right hand is held facing down with the wrist bent and fingertips and thumb close together, representing a bell shape. The palm of the open left hand strikes the "bell" twice.

BIG

The side-held hands move away from each other, showing the large size of something. Note the extended, bent forefingers and raised thumbs.

BIRD

The index finger and thumb are held close to the mouth and open and close like a bird's beak.

228

BLACK

The tip of the index finger is drawn across the forehead, indicating black eyebrows.

BLANKET

The downturned hands grasp and pull up an imaginary blanket.

229

BLUE

Make a "B" hand shape by holding up your flat hand with your fingers together and your thumb bent inward across your palm. Shake your "B" in the space off the right shoulder. (This is the area where some color signs are made.)

BOAT

Cup your hands together to form a little "boat" and make it move away from you with a rolling motion, like a boat moving through the water.

BOOK

Hold the hands flat, palms together. Open hands like the covers of a book.

BRUSH HAIR

Mimic the act of holding the handle of a brush and brushing hair.

BUBBLES

The cupped hands mimic catching bubbles in the air and popping them.

BUG

The thumb rests on the end of the nose while the first two fingers wiggle, like the antennae of an insect.

BUILD

The hands show things being stacked up on top of each other.

BUS

Non-ASL version
The two fists mimic steering a large, low-down steering wheel. This is similar to **CAR**, but with the fist held horizontally on a bigger steering wheel. **BUS** is most commonly fingerspelled in ASL, so this isn't an official ASL sign.

ASL version
Pull an imaginary cord with your first two fingers bent. This is a fun but lesser-known sign. It's used in the *Signing Time* videos, which I love.

BUTTERFLY

The hands fly around with the thumbs locked against each and the fingers wiggling, representing a butterfly fluttering about.

CAR

The two fists mimic the steering of a car.

CAREFUL

Repeat the sign for KEEP: Bounce one "K" hand on top of the other at an angle, twice. ("K" is signed by holding up the first two fingers with the middle finger slanted in at an angle.)

CAT

The thumb and index finger come together at the upper lip and move outward and away from the face as if sliding whiskers through the fingers. You can use one or both hands.

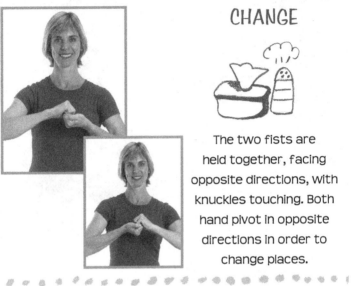

CHANGE

The two fists are held together, facing opposite directions, with knuckles touching. Both hand pivot in opposite directions in order to change places.

CLEAN
(NOT DIRTY)

One flat palm wipes dirt off of the other flat palm.

CLOTHES

The open hands move down in front of the body, the tips of the thumbs just skimming the chest, indicating clothing hanging from the body.

CLOUDS

The open hands are held up and turn inward repeatedly, outlining the puffy shape of clouds.

COLD

The shoulders are hunched
and the clenched hands
shake, as if shivering
with cold.

COMB HAIR

Comb hair with fingers.

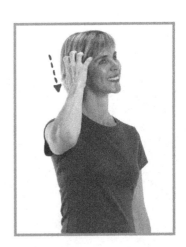

COOKIE

Mimic cutting out a cookie with a cookie cutter: The action hand, held in a "claw" shape, twists around and back again against the opposite flat palm, as if cutting through dough.

COW

The thumbs of the "Y" hand rest on the temples, then bend forward at the wrist. Can also be done one-handed.

CRACKER

The fist of the base hand is held against the opposite shoulder, as the action hand forms a fist and strikes the elbow of the base arm several times.

DADDY

The thumb of the sideways "5" hand taps the middle of the forehead several times. The fingertips may wiggle.

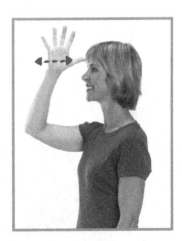

DANCE

The first two fingers of the action hand form an inverted "V" and swing rhythmically back and forth over the upturned palm of the base hand.

DANGER

Both fists are held closed in the "A" hand shape. One hand thrusts up suddenly, brushing past the other fist, representing something happening suddenly and unexpectedly.

DIAPER.

Both hands are held at the hips as the first two fingers open and close on the thumbs, indicating diaper pins opening and closing.

DIRTY

Hold hand under chin and wiggle fingers. (You're in dirt up to your neck!)

DOG

The hand pats the knee
and/or snaps the fingers,
as if calling a dog.

DOLL

The bent forefinger
is pulled twice down
the nose.

DOWN

The natural gesture—the index finger points down.

DRY

The index finger drags across the chin as if drying it.

DUCK

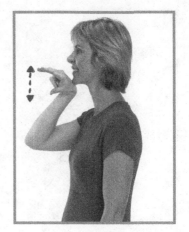

The hand is held near the mouth, facing out, while the first two fingers open and close on top of the thumb, indicating a duck's bill.

EAT

The fingers and thumb, held together as if grasping a small piece of food, tap the mouth several times.

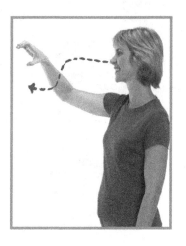

ELEPHANT

Starting at the nose,
the "C" hand traces the
shape of an elephant's
trunk.

FALL DOWN

The first two fingers
make an upside-down
"V" on the opposite hand,
representing a person
standing. Then they "fall"
off the hand.

FAN

The index finger is held up, turning around and around, representing the motion of a fan.

FINISHED
(ALL DONE)

Both "5" hands are held with the palms up, and then they flip over in one swift motion.

FIRE TRUCK

Sign **FIRE** by alternately raising each hand and wriggling the fingers to represent flickering flames. Then sign **TRUCK** by pretending to steer a big steering wheel.

FISH

Hold your hand on its side and make it "swim" away from you, like a fish moving through the water.

FLOWER

The fingers and thumb of action hand are held together, as if grasping a tiny flower by the stem. The hand moves from one side of the nose to the other, as if smelling the flower.

FRUIT

Pinch your index finger and thumb together at the corner of your mouth in the "F" hand shape, then twist as if you're twisting the stem off a cherry that's in your mouth.

FUN

Hold the first two fingers of the action hand together in the "U" hand shape. Brush them against the tip of your nose, then bring them down on the first two fingers of the base hand, which are also held in the "U" hand shape.

FUNNY

The first two fingers are held in the "U" hand shape and brush against the end of your nose, as if you're tickling someone's nose with a feather to make them laugh.

GIRAFFE

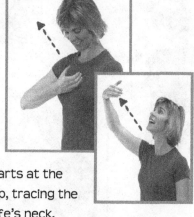

The "C" hand starts at the neck and moves up, tracing the shape of giraffe's neck.

GIVE

The thumb and fingers are held together, as if grasping something, and the hand moves away from the signer, as if giving something away. You can use one or both hands.

251

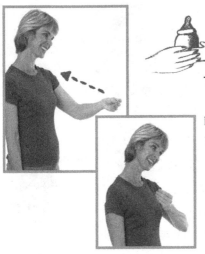

GIVE ME

The thumb and fingers
are held together, as
if grasping something.
The hand starts some
distance away from
the body and then
moves in closer, as if
taking something
from someone.

GLASSES

The thumbs and index
fingers indicate the outline
of glasses.

GO

Both hands, with index
fingers extended, bend
at the wrists and point
in the direction you're
going.

GRANDMA

The "5" hand is held
sideways with the thumb
touching the chin. The hand
then moves downward and
away in two arcs (similar
to **MOMMY,** but with two
arcs that symbolize two
generations).

GRANDPA

The "5" hand is held sideways with the thumb touching the forehead. The hand then moves downward and away in two arcs (similar to **DADDY,** but with two arcs that symbolize two generations).

GRASS

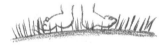

The hand moves with the palm up under the chin and brushes the underside of the chin twice. This represents an animal eating hay or grass.

GREEN

Make a "G" hand shape by holding your hand sideways with your thumb and forefinger almost touching, as if you're about to pinch something. Shake the "G" hand in the space off the right shoulder. (This is the area where some color signs are made.)

HAPPY

The flat hand pats the chest repeatedly with an upward stroking movement, representing happy feelings bubbling up.

255

HAT

Pat your head, showing where your hat goes.

HEAR

The natural gesture—the index finger points to the ear. You may observe your baby doing this naturally in response to sounds, even before you demonstrate it.

HELICOPTER

Hold up the thumb and the first two fingers of the base hand to make a "3" hand. Place the open action hand palm down on the thumb and make it quiver as both rise.

HELP

ASL version: The action hand, formed into a fist, is placed on top of the flat base hand. Both rise up together as if the flat hand is helping lift the fist. The thumb may point upward and can be used to indicate who needs help by pointing as it rises.

Non-ASL version: This is recommended for very young children by Joseph Garcia in *Sign with Your Baby*. Both flat hands pat the chest, which is easier for parents to recognize when done by younger babies.

HIDE

The thumbnail of the "A" hand touches the chin, then swoops down to hide under the opposite downturned palm.

HIPPOPOTAMUS

Extend the index and little fingers of each hand to form two "Y" hand shapes. Make the hands open and close on each other like a big mouth opening. The extended fingers are the hippo's big teeth.

HOME

The fingers and thumb, brought together to form a flattened "O," move from side of the mouth to the cheek. This is a variation of **EAT** and **SLEEP.**

HOORAY!
(also "YIPPEE!" "YAHOO!" and "YEAH!")

Raise both open hands up in the air and shake them as you cheer "Hooray!" This is the ASL version of applause. The whole point of clapping your hands is to make the loud noise—but that misses the point if you're deaf. Hence, the raised-hands-shaking sign means **HOORAY!**

HORSE

The thumb touches the
temple, while the extended
first two fingers flap up
and down together, like a
horses ear. You can use
one or both hands.

HOT

The signer nolds the
hand like a claw with
the palm facing the
mouth, then drops the
palm downward, as if
spitting out hot food and
throwing it on the floor.

HOUSE

The flat hands describe
the outline of a house
with a pointed roof.

IN

One hand pretends to put
something in the other.

JUMP

The first two fingers of the action hand form an inverted "V" on the palm of the base hand. The action hand springs up and down, representing legs jumping.

KEYS

The index finger of the action hand bends at the knuckle and turns in the sideways palm of the base hand, representing a key turning in a lock.

LIGHT
(ON/OFF/FLASHING)

The raised hand bends down at the wrist with tips of fingers and thumb held together. The fingers then open, representing rays of light shining down.

Variations: Fingers open means **LIGHT ON.** Fingers closed means **LIGHT OFF.** Both hands open and closing repeatedly and quickly means **FLASHING LIGHTS.**

LION

Bend your fingers to make a "claw hand" and sweep your hand from the front of your head to the back, outlining the mane of a lion.

LITTLE

The sideways-held hands moves toward and away from each other, indicating that something is small.

LOOK

The first two fingers form a "V," pointing at the eyes, then move away toward what you're looking at.

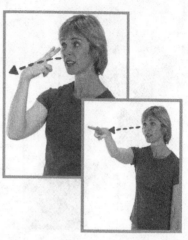

+

LOUD

Combine the signs **HEAR** and **SHAKE** to mean the sound was so loud that it shook the ground!

MILK

The sideways-held fist is opened and closed several times, as if milking a cow.

MOMMY

The thumb of sideways "5" hand taps the chin several times. The fingertips may wiggle.

MONKEY

The hands scratch up and down on the sides of the body, imitating a monkey.

MOON

A modified "C" hand is made with the thumb and forefinger. It taps the temple, then rises up over the head as the signer gazes up at it.

MORE

The thumbs and fingertips of each hand are held together, and the fingertips of both hands tap together several times. This represents gathering more things together.

MOUSE

The fist is held in front of the chin as the extended index finger brushes across the nose several times, indicating a mouse's twitching nose.

MUSIC

The action hand, held on its side, moves rhythmically back and forth over the forearm, which is held in front of the chest.

NO

The first two fingers close down on the thumb. This is a variation of the finger spelling of no.

OFF

One flat hand moves off
of the other.

ON

One flat hand moves
onto the other.

ORANGE
(color or fruit)

Pretend to squeeze the juice from an orange into your mouth.

OUT/ OUTSIDE

For **OUT,** one hand moves out of the other. For **OUTSIDE,** repeat the motion.

271

PAIN

The two index fingers tap together
several times at the location of
the pain, representing throbbing nerve
endings. The face should show
a pained expression.

EARACHE

This is an example of
localizing the sign at the
site of the pain.

PANTS

Go through the motion
of pulling up pants.

PINK

The "P" hand shape points
to the lips and then
moves downward.
(This is similar to RED.)

PLAY

Raise the thumbs and pinkies of both hands to form a "Y" hand shape. Shake hands, pivoting at the wrists, representing the shaking of a tambourine.

PLEASE

The open palm touches the chest and moves in a circular motion.

POOP

Pull the thumb out of
the bottom of the
opposite closed fist.

PRAY

The hands are held in a
gesture of prayer.

PROUD

The thumb of the "A" hand moves up the chest, indicating the feeling of pride welling up inside.

PURPLE

Make a "P" hand shape by drooping your pointer finger downward at an angle, then shake your "P" hand in the area off your right shoulder. (This is the area where some color signs are made.)

PURSE

The signer mimes holding a purse by the handle and bouncing it up and down a couple of times.

RABBIT (BUNNY)

Raise the first two fingers, holding them together in the "U" hand shape. Hold them at your temples and make them twitch back a couple of times. You can use one or both hands.

277

RAIN

The hands are held palms down with fingers spread and bent. They make a double downward movement, representing rain falling.

RATTLE

The hand mimics shaking a rattle.

READ

The first two fingers form a "V," representing the eyes, which scan the flat palm of the opposite hand, as if "reading" it.

RED

The index finger points to the lips and then moves downward, indicating the red color of the lips.

ROLL

The index fingers roll over one another as they move forward.

SEE

The first two fingers form a "V," representing the eyes. They move forward to show the concept of seeing. (Also see **LOOK.**)

SHAKE

The two fists move back and forth as if shaking something.

SHAMPOO

The fingers go through the motion of massaging shampoo into the scalp.

281

SHEEP

Make the first two fingers of your right hand into an imaginary pair of scissors and clip "wool" off of your left downturned arm.

SHIRT

Indicate the shirt by pulling on the front of it. You can use one or both hands.

SHOES

The thumb sides of the fists tap together, representing someone clicking the heels of their shoes together.

SIGN

The upward-pointing index fingers move in alternating circles toward the signer, representing the movement of the hands while signing.

SILLY

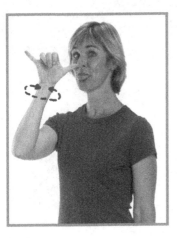

Raise the thumb and little finger to make a "Y" hand shape. Twist it in front of your face, brushing the thumb against your nose.

SIT

The first two fingers of the action hand form a "V," and then bend at the knuckles to "sit" on the first two fingers of the base hand.

SLIDE

The first two fingers of
the action hand are held in
a "V" shape, representing
legs. They slide down the
first two fingers of the
opposite hand, which are
held together, representing
a playground slide.

SNAKE

The first two fingers are
bent to look like the fangs
of a snake. The hand
moves down and away
from the mouth as it
curves back and forth like
a snake slithering.

SOAP

The fingertips move in
a circle in the palm of
the opposite hand, as if
lathering soap.

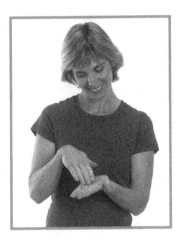

SOCKS

The index fingers point
downward and alternately
run against each other, like
knitting needles making
socks.

SPLASH

The fists are brought together in front of the body, then move up- and outward as the fingers splay open with palms facing out to represent a big splash.

STARS

The two index fingers rub against each other as they point alternately skyward. This represents stars twinkling.

287

STOP

The edge of one hand comes down on the palm of the other, representing something coming to an abrupt stop.

STORE/ SELL

The fingers and thumbs are held together, making the flattened "O" hand shape. They point to the body, then move outward at the wrists. This represents holding up something you are selling.

If you do the wrist motion only once, it means **SELL;** repeated multiple times, it means **STORE.** When signing with hearing babies, we tend to repeat motions a lot anyway, to ensure that they see our signs, but it's good to know this difference for your own information.

SUN

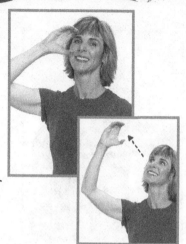

The "C" hand taps the temple, then rises up over the head as the signer gazes up at it.

SWING

The first two fingers of one hand form an inverted "V" and bend to sit on the first two fingers of the opposite hand. Both move back and forth in an arc like a person on a swing.

TELEPHONE

The "Y" hand is held to the side of the head like a telephone

TELL (SAY)

The index finger starts at the chin and moves away, representing the flow of words coming out of the mouth.

THANK YOU/ YOU'RE WELCOME

The fingertips of the flat hand touch the lips and then move out and down toward the person being thanked, representing nice words coming from the mouth.

THROW

The hand starts near the face with the fingertips and thumb together in a flattened "O" hand shape. The hand then opens as it moves forward, as if throwing something.

TIGER

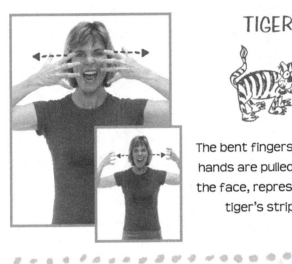

The bent fingers of both hands are pulled across the face, representing a tiger's stripes.

TOOTHBRUSH (BRUSH TEETH)

The signer mimes brushing teeth with index finger.

TOUCH

The middle finger drops down to touch the back of the opposite hand.

TOWEL

Pretend to pull an imaginary towel back and forth behind you, as if drying your back.

TOY

Make two fists with your thumbs between your first two fingers; these are "T" hands. Shake your "T" hands.

TRACTOR

Pretend to grasp a steering wheel, as in **CAR,** then bounce your entire body as if driving a tractor over bumpy ground.

TRAIN

Both hands are held in the "U" or "V" hand shape, the fingers of one hand moving back and forth on the fingers of the other, representing the tracks and railway ties.

TREE

The elbow of the action hand rests on the opposite open palm with fingers splayed open (the "5" hand) to represent the branches of a tree. The hand pivots back and forth at the wrist.

TRUCK

The two fists mimic driving a large steering wheel. This is similar to **CAR,** but lower down and with a bigger steering wheel.

UP

The natural gesture—the index finger points up.

VEGETABLE

The first two fingers form a "V" hand shape and twist at the side of the mouth.

WAIT

One hand is held slightly in front of the other as the fingers flutter.

WANT

Extend the fingers of
both hands forward with your
palms up, then pull
back as your fingers
close, as if pulling
something toward
yourself. Many babies
do this sign naturally,

WARM

The closed fist is held close
to the mouth and then
opens as it moves away,
representing warm breath
coming from the mouth.

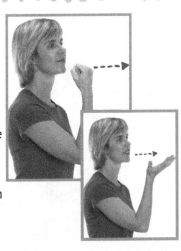

WASH (CLEAN UP)

The closed fist scrubs the opposite open palm in a circular motion, as if washing something.

WASH HANDS

Rub hands all over each other, as if washing them.

WATER

The first 3 fingers form a "W" and tap the chin twice.

WET

The ASL sign for **WET** combines the signs for **WATER** with **SOFT,** which is made by opening and closing the fingers.

For simplicity's sake, you might sometimes abbreviate it and just do the opening-and-closing-fingers part, as if you're feeling the wetness on your fingertips. I especially like to do this when I'm singing a song to my children that uses the **WET** sign.

WHAT

The hands are raised with the palms up, in the natural "What?" gesture.

WHERE

The hand, with the index finger extended, waves from side to side in a small arc.

WHITE

The open palm is placed against the chest and then pulled straight out as the fingertips come together.

WIND

Both open hands are held sideways in front of the body. The hands sway gracefully from side to side like trees blowing in the wind.

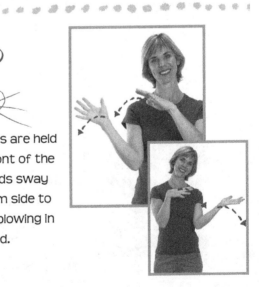

WORK

Form both hands into "S" hand shapes by making fists with the thumbs lying across the knuckles. With the palms facing down, tap one wrist on the other a few times, as if hammering.

YELLOW

Make a "Y" hand by raising only your thumb and pinkie. Shake the "Y" hand to the right in the space off your right shoulder. (This is the area where some color signs are made.)

YUMMY
(DELICIOUS)

The middle finger touches the lip, then brushes against the thumb as it moves outward in a motion similar to snapping your fingers.

My niece Ruby signs ICE CREAM.

appendix

resources

Baby Sign Language Books

Sign with Your Baby Complete Learning Kit, by Joseph Garcia (Northlight Communications, Seattle, WA, 1999). This kit includes the book *Sign with Your Baby* (which includes 145 ASL signs), an instructional video, and a laminated reference chart. The components of the kit can also be purchased separately. Please visit: **www.sign2me.com.**

Signing Smart with Babies and Toddlers, by Michelle Anthony M.A., Ph.D. and Reyna Lindert, Ph.D. (St. Martin's Press, New York, NY, 2005) Anthony and Lindert's Signing Smart method is a simple, straightforward, and intelligent ASL method for signing with babies, and is compatible with other ASL methods. The book contains many fun signing activities and songs.

Baby Signs: How to Talk with Your Baby Before Your Baby Can Talk, by Linda Acredolo, Ph.D., and Susan Goodwyn, Ph.D., with Douglas Abrams (McGraw Hill/Contemporary Books, Columbus, OH, 2002). Drs. Acredolo and Goodwyn conducted a long-term study on using signing with hearing babies, funded by the National Institutes of Health and

Human Development. This book contains their findings, developmental information, strategies, and activities. There's only one drawback: Purists should be aware that many of the signs included aren't actual ASL signs.

Dancing with Words: Signing for Hearing Children's Literacy, by Marilyn Daniels (Bergin & Garvey, Westport, CT, 2000). This book focuses on how signing with children enhances literacy and reading skills.

ASL Dictionaries

Teach Your Tot to Sign by Stacy A. Thompson, Valerie Nelson-Metlay (Illustrator) Gallaudet University Press (April 29, 2005). This wonderful little book is actually a complete baby sign language dictionary of over 500 signs appropriate for babies through preschoolers!

Signs for Me: Basic Sign Vocabulary for Children, Parents, and Teachers, by Ben Bahan and Joe Dannis (DawnSignPress, San Diego, CA, 1990). This book of kid-friendly signs is organized grammatically and thematically. The signers in the pictures are children, and the large images are suitable for coloring.

Random House Webster's American Sign Language Dictionary, by Elaine Costello (Random House, New York, NY, 1999). Available in full, concise, and pocket versions. The pocket one is the best because of its tiny size and *plastic cover*—don't leave home without it!

American Sign Language Dictionary, by Martin L.A. Sternberg (HarperCollins, New York, NY, 1998). This is available in full or concise versions.

Children's Books

Amazon.com has the widest selection.

Animal Signs: A First Book of Sign Language, by Debby Slier (Gallaudet University Press, Washington, D.C., 1995). This board book contains illustrations and corresponding signs.

Baby's First Signs and More Baby's First Signs, by Kim Votry and Kurt Waller (Gallaudet University Press, Washington, D.C., 2001). These are beautiful board books!

Word Signs: A First Book of Sign Language, by Debby Slier (Gallaudet University Press, Washington, D.C., 1995). This board book contains object photos and corresponding signs.

Opposites: A Beginner's Book of Signs and *Happy Birthday: A Beginner's Book of Signs,* by Angela Bednarczyk, et al. (Star Bright Books, Long Island City, NY, 1997). This board book contains object photos and corresponding signs.
My First Book of Sign Language, by Joan Holub (Troll Assoc., Memphis, TN, 1998).

Simple Signs, by Cindy Wheeler (Puffin, London, England, 1997).

You Can Learn Sign Language!: More Than 300 Words in Pictures, by Jackie Kramer, et al. (Troll Assoc., Memphis, TN, 2000).

An Alphabet of Animal Signs, by S. Harold Collins, et al. (Garlic Press, Eugene, OR, 2001). This book contains an animal sign for each letter of the alphabet.

Pets, Animals & Creatures by Jane Phillips, et al. (Garlic Press, Eugene, OR, 2001). This contains photos and signs for 77 pets, farm animals, and wild animals. Garlic Press has many other wonderful signing books for children; check out: **www.garlicpress.com.**

My First Baby Signs; Baby Signs for Mealtime; Baby Signs for Animals; and *Baby Signs for Bedtime,* by Linda Acredolo, et al. (HarperFestival, New York, NY, 2002). These board books feature cute signing baby photos (but they're not all ASL signs).

Videos

Signing Time!: Volumes 1–12 and *Baby Signing Time!: Volumes 1 and 2,* by Two Little Hands Productions (Salt Lake City, UT, 2002/2004). These are amazing children's videos and DVDs (*Baby Signing Time!* is DVD only)—they're "must-haves"! *Signing Time!* features a deaf child and her younger hearing cousin, and *Baby Signing Time!* features an animated baby and her hearing cousin. I have to say that these are the very best children's entertainment I've ever seen, signing or not. They're wonderful quality with beautiful original music, and show lots of children of all ages and abilities using signs. Check out: **www.signingtime.com.**

Sign with your Baby, by Northlight Communications (Seattle, WA, 1999). This is an instructional video for adults.

Sign Songs, by Education 2000 (1998). This instructional video features favorite children's songs.

Blue's Clues: All Kinds of Signs, by Paramount Studio (Hollywood, CA, 2001).

Sign-Me-a-Story, by Sony Wonder (1987).

Talking Hands: A Sign Language Video for Children, by Small Fry Productions (Alpharetta, GA, 2001).

Baby See 'n Sign: Volume 1, by Kronz Kidz Productions (Creswell, OR, 2001). This is an excellent learning video with more than 60 signs for babies and toddlers.

Baby See 'n Sign: Volume 2, by Kronz Kidz Productions (Creswell, OR, 2003).

The Treasure Chest, by Wide-Eyed Learning (Portland, OR, and Denver, CO, 2003). This is an engaging and educational video for children and adults. Please visit: **www. wideeyedlearning.com.**

Music

Pick Me Up! by Northlight Communications (Seattle, WA, 2003). This set includes a music CD and hardcover activity guide with tear-resistant pages. It contains wonderful children's music that won't grate on your nerves, in styles like Sinatra, the Beach Boys, Elvis, and more. Available at: **www.sign2me.com**

Other Media

Reminder Series Poster/Placemats by Northlight Communications (Seattle, WA, 2002). These are laminated posters in eight themes, with 12 signing concepts per theme. Each poster presents concepts in ASL, English, and Spanish and are the perfect size for using as place mats or posting on walls. They're available at: **www.sign2me.com.**

endnotes

Chapter 1

    1. *Baby Signs,* Linda Acredolo, Ph.D., and Susan Goodwyn, Ph.D.

Chapter 3

    1. *Sign with your Baby,* Joseph Garcia.

    2. "Making Every Sign Count," Patricia Spencer, Ph.D., *Perspectives in Education and Deafness,* Vol. 17, #2.

    3. *Signing Smart with Babies and Toddlers,* Michelle Anthony, M.A., Ph.D., and Reyna Lindert, Ph.D.

thanks!

acknowledgments

I'd like to thank Joseph Garcia for his pioneering research in using sign language with hearing babies, and the entire staff of Sign2Me/Northlight Communications for all their incredible support and encouragement in getting my classes up and running and in writing my own books. I'd also like to thank all of my fellow Sign2Me presenters and signing parents who generously donated their wonderful and imaginative contributions to this book. Last but not least, I want to thank Gwen Cox, Echo Greenlee, and all the members of the Sign2Me (aka Sign with Your Baby) Presenters' Network for continually sharing ideas, encouragement, and support. It's so wonderful to be on this adventure with all of you as we bring the magic of communication to parents and children the world over!

about the author

Monta Briant, a native of San Francisco, and her husband, Paul, of Cape Town, South Africa, began signing with their daughter, Sirena, when she was six months old. The family eventually learned hundreds of signs together. Monta was so moved by the experience of being able to communicate effectively with her then-preverbal daughter that she found herself telling anyone pushing a stroller about baby sign language.

In 2001, Monta, a former professional yacht captain, decided to make a permanent career change that would enable her to stay home with her daughter, and she founded Baby Sign Language Workshops. An enthusiastic speaker and self-proclaimed "Baby Sign Language evangelist," Monta teaches workshops and parent-tot signing classes throughout San Diego County and is also available for speaking engagements. Her programs have been the subject of feature stories in The San Diego Union-Tribune and on Fox 6 News, KUSI News, and KPBS's Full Focus.

In 2004, the Briants welcomed baby brother Aiden to the family and began signing with him immediately. Big sister Sirena, now age four, still remembers her signs and is helping to teach her brother.

Monta is a member of the Sign with Your Baby™ Presenters' Network and can be reached at **Monta@ babysignlanguage.net.** For class schedules and other information, please visit: **www.babysignlanguage.net.**

We hope you enjoyed this Hay House book. If you'd like to receive our online catalog featuring additional information on Hay House books and products, or if you'd like to find out more about the Hay Foundation, please contact:

Hay House, Inc., P.O. Box 5100, Carlsbad, CA 92018-5100
(760) 431-7695 or (800) 654-5126
(760) 431-6948 (fax) or (800) 650-5115 (fax)
www.hayhouse.com® • www.hayfoundation.org

———

Published in Australia by: Hay House Australia Pty. Ltd.,
18/36 Ralph St., Alexandria NSW 2015
Phone: 612-9669-4299 • *Fax:* 612-9669-4144
www.hayhouse.com.au

Published in the United Kingdom by: Hay House UK, Ltd.,
The Sixth Floor, Watson House, 54 Baker Street, London W1U 7BU
Phone: +44 (0)20 3927 7290 • *Fax:* +44 (0)20 3927 7291
www.hayhouse.co.uk

Published in India by: Hay House Publishers India,
Muskaan Complex, Plot No. 3, B-2, Vasant Kunj, New Delhi 110 070
Phone: 91-11-4176-1620 • *Fax:* 91-11-4176-1630
www.hayhouse.co.in

———

Access New Knowledge.
Anytime. Anywhere.

Learn and evolve at your own pace
with the world's leading experts.

www.hayhouseU.com

Printed in the United States
by Baker & Taylor Publisher Services